VITAL GUIDE

FIGHTING SHIPS OF WORLD WAR II

LEO MARRIOTT

Airlife

Contents

Introduction

This book sets out to describe the major warships of the great naval powers engaged in the bitter struggles of World War II. On the Allied side these comprised the fleets of Britain and the Commonwealth nations, together with the United States and France, which were ranged against the Axis navies of Germany, Italy and Japan. There were, of course, numerous other navies involved at various times but it is not possible to include a description of these forces in a book of this size. The following very brief outline of the naval war between 1939 and 1945 is intended to give a broad backdrop against which the role of the various navies and their warships can be assessed.

The German invasion of Poland on 1 September 1939 was swiftly followed on 3 September by declarations of war by France and Great Britain. The German Navy was numerically very small and, although its ships were modern and well armed, it could not hope to engage in traditionally large set-piece battles but instead concentrated its efforts on the vital sealanes that supplied the Allies with foodstuffs and the materials of war. Although surface raiders were used for this purpose, it was the U-boat that caused the most damage and these remained a constant menace right up to the end of hostilities in May 1945, despite the Battle of the Atlantic effectively having been won by the Allies in May 1943. France initially co-operated with British forces, including the unsuccessful attempt to prevent the German invasion of Norway in April 1940. However, the defeat of the French armies at home in June 1940 led to the neutralisation of most of the French fleet and it was subsequently scuttled at Toulon in November 1942, although a number of other ships did eventually rejoin the Allied forces. The German invasion of Russia in May 1941 led to the institution of supply convoys through the Arctic oceans, and these were the trigger for a number of bloody engagements between British and German forces off the Norwegian coast. Operation Overlord, the great amphibious invasion of northern France in June 1944, spelt the beginning of the end for Germany which, pressed by the Allied armies in the west and the Russians in the east, was eventually defeated in May 1945.

Italy entered the war on the Axis side in July 1940 following the fall of France, and the Mediterranean became a major theatre of naval operations until the successful invasions of North Africa in November 1942 and Sicily and Italy in 1943 brought about the Italian surrender. Meanwhile the United States was dragged into the war by the Japanese attack on Pearl Harbor in December 1941. Initially, the Japanese swept all before them and ranged across the Pacific and Indian oceans destroying American, British and Dutch forces as they went. The turning point came in the Battle of Midway in July 1942, but it took another three years for Allied forces to fight their way back through south-east Asia and across the Pacific to the point where they were poised for an invasion of the Japanese homeland. The need for this operation, which was forecast to result in up to a million casualties, was swept away by the dropping of two atomic bombs in August 1945, and this effectively brought hostilities to an end. Appropriately, the Japanese surrender was accepted and signed aboard an American battleship, the USS *New Jersey*.

In this book, the major warships of the main combatant navies are described. These include battleships and battle-cruisers, aircraft carriers, cruisers, destroyers and escort vessels, and submarines. Each of these types is grouped together in sections so that comparisons can be made between similar vessels from different navies. Within each section the Allied navies (Britain, United States and France) are described first, followed by the Axis navies of Germany, Italy and Japan. Space does not permit the inclusion of the many smaller craft including corvettes, coastal forces and patrol vessels, all of which had important roles to play, nor the great variety of support and auxiliary vessels without which the front-line fleets could not have functioned. Amphibious warfare also spawned a whole family of specialised ships and craft that regrettably cannot be covered in this volume either.

BATTLESHIPS AND BATTLECRUISERS

At the outbreak of war in 1939 the battleship was still seen as the main instrument of naval power. Although the threat from aircraft was not ignored, their ability to sink heavily armoured warships under battle conditions was not proven and all the major navies were building a new breed of fast battleship. However, by 1939 very few of these had been completed; the majority of the world's capital ships had been built or laid down during World War I (1914–18). During that conflict, although the aeroplane and submarine had come to maturity, the position of the battleship had not been seriously challenged, and by 1921 Britain, Japan and the United States were considering the construction of new super battleships armed with 18in (457mm) or 16in (406mm) guns and displacing over 48,000 tons. However, these construction programmes would be very expensive and the political climate demanded a reduction in world armaments after the Armageddon of the Great War. Consequently the United States convened the Washington Naval Conference in 1921 and the resulting treaty was to have a major effect on warship construction programmes for the next 20 years.

The immediate result of this treaty was that a large number of older battleships were scrapped and some under construction were also abandoned. However, Japan was permitted to complete two 16in battleships then under construction while the United States was also allowed to do the same with three Colorado class battleships launched in 1921. In order to maintain parity, Britain was therefore permitted to lay down two new battleships (*Nelson* and *Rodney*) also armed with 16in guns. At the 1931 London Naval Conference, the suspension of battleship construction was extended to 1937, but France and Italy did not agree to this and laid down Dunkerque class battlecruisers and Littorio class battleships in the mid-1930s, although with 13in (330mm) and 15in (381mm) guns respectively they otherwise complied with the qualitative provisions established at the Washington conference. In 1934 Japan gave two years' formal notice of their intention to withdraw from the treaty provisions and Italy refused to accept further restrictions. Another London conference in 1935 achieved little, although Britain proposed that capital ship main armament should be limited to 14in (355mm) guns, subject to agreement by all the original treaty signatories. This did not happen, and in any case Japan announced in 1937 that she would no longer observe the 35,000-ton limit. Finally, in 1938, the other signatories agreed that the limits on battleship size should be increased to 45,000 tons and main armament to 16in guns. By this time such limits were academic as all nations were building new battleships and many of these were already in excess of the previous limitations. Thus Italy and France had produced the Littorio and Richelieu classes each armed with 15in guns and nominally within the 35,000-ton limit. Britain and the United States also built down to the displacement limit with the King George V and Washington class battleships, although the former had the self-imposed 14in guns while the Americans went for the 16in gun which also armed all their subsequent battleships. Germany, while arming the new *Bismarck* and *Tirpitz* with 15in guns, had deliberately and substantially exceeded the 35,000-ton limit, and Japan was engaged on the construction of three 64,000-ton monsters armed with 18in guns.

Thanks to improvements in propulsive efficiency and longer hulls, all of the new battleships were capable of around 30kt and consequently the traditional concept of the heavily armed but lightly armoured fast battlecruiser became redundant. Although Germany, France and the United States did still build battlecruisers, they tended to have a lighter main armament while still having adequate armour protection and the speed to operate with the new battleships.

Nevertheless, very few of the new ships were completed prior to 1939, and at the outbreak of war the majority of capital ships were over 20 years old and had been designed to cope with the hazards of an earlier era. In the period between the two world wars, the aeroplane had matured as a weapon system and posed a much more potent threat, although it was still thought in most naval circles that a well-armed battleship could successfully fight off such attacks. However, if they were to do this the older battleships needed substantial improvements to their anti-aircraft armament and many were modernised to varying degrees in the late 1930s. The most extensive modernisation programmes produced ships that were virtually the equivalent of the newer battleships in almost every respect except speed. The most outstanding examples of this process were perhaps the Italian Conte de Cavour class and the British Queen Elizabeth class, while many older American battleships were substantially modernised after being damaged at Pearl Harbor in 1941.

Following the outbreak of hostilities in 1939 the battleship was still regarded as the core of any fleet, although it quickly became apparent that they were more likely to suffer attack from the air than from other capital ships. Nevertheless there were a number of surface actions involving battleships, perhaps the most famous and dramatic being the pursuit of the German battleship *Bismarck* by British forces. The initial action was an entirely conventional gunnery engagement during which the German ship sank the battlecruiser *Hood* with only a few salvoes and damaged the modern and untried HMS *Prince of Wales*. The *Bismarck* was eventually slowed down by a brave and fortunate airborne torpedo strike which enabled HMS *King George V* and HMS *Rodney* to close and finish her off with gunfire.

In November 1940, British carrier-based aircraft launched a successful strike against the Italian fleet at Taranto and seriously damaged three battleships. The Japanese took this form of attack a stage further in December 1941 with their dramatic raid on Pearl Harbor as a result of which several US battleships were seriously damaged and one was a total loss. Although these actions involved the use of aircraft, there were still those who held that modern battleships, properly handled in open waters, could defend themselves against concentrated air attack and were therefore still capable of independent deployment. This myth was ended on 10 December 1941 when Japanese torpedo bombers attacked and sank the British battleship *Prince of Wales* and battlecruiser *Repulse* off the coast of Malaya. This finally brought to an end the battleship's traditional role as the arbiter of seapower and thereafter they were mainly used as part of a force centred around one or more aircraft carriers, or to support amphibious landings where their awesome firepower could be put to good use.

No new battleships were laid down after 1941 (apart from the US Montana class, which were subsequently cancelled) although two, *Jean Bart* (France) and HMS *Vanguard* (Britain), were not completed until after the end of World War II. Of those that survived the war, most were quickly decommissioned and eventually scrapped, although for reasons of national prestige or for specialised tasks a few remained in service for several decades after 1945.

UNITED KINGDOM
Queen Elizabeth

HMS Queen Elizabeth *as modernised. (Sydney Goodman Collection)*

These five battleships were far and away the best produced by Britain in World War I and were naturally retained after 1918. During the 1920s they were modernised to some extent, the most obvious external change being the trunking together of the two funnels into one broad funnel amidships. Other changes included the fitting of external bulges to improve protection and the additional 4in (102mm) AA guns in lieu of deck-mounted 6in (153mm) guns. However, in the 1930s a much more substantial modernisation programme was devised which would ensure that these ships were capable of meeting the greatly increased threat of air attack, as well as improving their surface warfare capability.

In fact, the degree of modernisation actually implemented varied considerably, and consequently, there were major differences between the various ships by 1939. The least altered was *Barham*, which was refitted 1931–4, and changes were limited to an increase in light AA armament, improved gunnery control arrangements and the fitting of an aircraft catapult on the roof of X turret. *Malaya* underwent similar changes but had a hangar and athwartships catapult fitted abaft the funnel. In both cases the modifications increased displacement and consequently speed was reduced. However, the next to be modernised, *Warspite*, underwent a much more fundamental rebuild between 1934 and 1937: she was fitted with new lightweight machinery, the range of the main armament was increased, an entirely new bridge and forward superstructure was built forward of the funnel and a hangar and catapult installed aft of the funnel. Some of the 6in guns were removed and additional 4in and multiple 2pdr mountings were fitted. Armour protection was also improved. Between 1937 and 1940, *Queen Elizabeth* and *Valiant* were also refitted along the lines of work carried out on *Warspite*, with the major difference that all 6in and 4in guns were removed and replaced with a homogeneous battery of 20 4.5in (114mm) DP guns in twin countersunk turrets, controlled by four HA directors.

Only one ship was lost during the war, the *Barham* being torpedoed by a German submarine in the eastern Mediterranean in November 1941. However, both *Queen Elizabeth* and *Valiant* were seriously damaged in an audacious attack by Italian frogmen while at anchor in Alexandria in December 1941 and were out of action for several months thereafter. *Warspite* had a particularly illustrious career and took part in many actions including Narvik, Calabria, Matapan and the Malta convoys. While supporting the landings at Salerno in September 1943 she was hit by a radio-controlled glider bomb which caused serious damage. Although she remained in service and subsequently supported operations in north-west Europe, she was not fully repaired and was eventually laid up early in 1945. All four remaining ships were scrapped shortly after World War II.

The Royal Navy also retained the five R class battleships after 1918 and, although laid down after the Queen Elizabeth class, they were slightly smaller and could make only 21kt at full load. They were not therefore modernised to any great extent and were mostly employed on second-line tasks such as convoy escort. *Royal Oak* was sunk while at anchor in Scapa Flow in October 1939 (an early German U-boat success) while *Royal Sovereign* was lent to the Soviet Navy in 1944 and was not returned until 1949. Those R class remaining with the Royal Navy were laid up in 1944 and all were scrapped in 1948–9.

HMS Warspite *was one of the most famous British battleships, with a distinguished career in two world wars. (Sydney Goodman Collection)*

SPECIFICATION

Class: Queen Elizabeth (battleship) Data *Queen Elizabeth* as modernised
Displacement: 31,585 tons (36,500 tons full load)
Length: 643ft (196m) oa
Beam: 90ft 6in (27.6m); 104ft (31.7m) across bulges
Draught: 35ft (10.7m) at full load
Machinery: 8 boilers, 4 shafts, Parsons SR geared turbines, 80,000shp
Speed: 24 kt
Range: 13,500nm (25,015km) at 10kt
Complement: 1,124+
Protection: Main belt 13in (330mm), upper belt 6in (152mm), end bulkheads 4/6in (102/152mm), funnel casing and uptakes 4in (102mm), decks 3.5in (89mm), over magazines 5in (127mm). Turrets 13in (330mm) on faces, 11in (279mm) sides, 5in (127mm) crowns, barbettes 6–10in (152–254mm). Hull bulges.
Armament: 8 15in/381mm (4 × 2), 20 4.5in/114mm DP (10 × 2), 32 2pdr AA (4 × 8), 16 0.5in/13mm AA (4 × 4).
Aircraft: 3. One catapult.
Ships in Class: *Queen Elizabeth* (1913), *Warspite* (1913), *Valiant* (1914), *Barham* (1914), *Malaya* (1915)

The battlecruiser HMS Hood *at anchor. (Sydney Goodman Collection)*

Between the wars, the battlecruiser HMS *Hood* represented the ultimate in British seapower. The largest capital ship in the world during the inter-war years, her long and handsome profile aroused excitement wherever she went. Completed in 1920, she led a Royal Navy squadron on a world cruise in 1923-4, visiting most of the countries which then comprised the British Empire.

As built, she introduced a number of novel features. For example, she was the first ship in the Royal Navy to incorporate an AC electrical supply, and the 5.5in (140 mm) guns which formed her secondary armament were unique at the time (one of these guns still survives as an obsolete coast defence weapon on Ascension Island in the mid-Atlantic). By 1939 some of these guns had been removed and the AA armament strengthened by the addition of twin 4in (102mm) AA mountings. There were plans to modernise her along the lines of the Queen Elizabeth class battleships and the battlecruiser *Renown* with the installation of new machinery and a dual purpose battery of 4.5in (114mm) guns replacing the existing 5.5in and 4in guns. The outbreak of war prevented this, and she remained attached to the Home Fleet and also took part in the unfortunate action against the French fleet at Oran in 1940. Subsequently she underwent a refit in late 1940 in which all the 5.5in guns were removed, the AA armament increased to 14 4in, and UP rocket projectors were fitted on B and Y turrets.

In this guise she was part of a force sent to intercept the heavily armed German battleship *Bismarck* and her escorting cruiser *Prinz Eugen* in May 1941. As Vice Admiral Holland raced towards the *Bismarck* in an attempt to close the range, the German gunnery was of its usual high standard and began to straddle the British ships. Even as the *Hood* and battleship *Prince of Wales* began to turn

so that their full armament could be brought to bear, the German ships scored a vital hit on the *Hood* which was suddenly rent by a massive explosion and sank within minutes leaving only three survivors from a crew of over 1,300 men. Controversy raged as to what was the exact cause of the explosion, but it is generally thought that the hit amidships ignited the ready use 4in ammunition and the resulting fires were communicated to the 4in magazines. Whatever the exact cause, there can rarely have been a more sudden and spectacular end to such a powerful warship.

SPECIFICATION

Class: Hood (battlecruiser) Data as May 1941
Displacement: 42,100 tons (46,200 tons full load)
Length: 810ft (246.9 m) pp, 861ft (262.4 m) oa
Beam: 95ft (29m); 105.25ft (32.1m) across bulges
Draught: 31.5ft (9.6m) full load
Machinery: 24 Yarrow boilers, 4 shafts, Brown-Curtiss turbines, 144,000shp
Speed: 31kt
Range: 6,300nm (11,673 km) at 12kt
Complement: 1,420
Protection: Main belt 5–12in (127–305mm), bulkheads 5–9in (127–229mm), decks 1.5–3in (38–76mm). Turrets 15in (381mm) face, 11–12in (229–305mm) sides, 5in (127mm) crowns. Barbettes 5–12in (127–305mm). External bulges.
Armament: Guns: 8 15in/381mm (4 × 2), 14 4in/102mm AA (6 × 2), 24 2pdr AA (3 × 8), 6 20mm/0.8in AA (6 × 1). Rockets: 5 20-barrelled UP rocket projectors. Torpedoes: 4 fixed 21in (533mm) torpedo tubes.
Aircraft: nil
Ships in Class: *Hood* (1918)

UNITED KINGDOM
Renown

A rare wartime view of HMS Repulse *in a disruptive camouflage scheme.* (Sydney Goodman Collection)

These two ships joined the fleet in 1916 after the Battle of Jutland had raised serious misgivings about the role of the battlecruiser. However, they were retained in the post-war fleet mainly because of their speed and the fact that they had proved to be good sea boats and steady gun platforms.

In the immediate post-war period their armour protection was increased, although there were some differences in the modifications made to each ship. As completed, both carried a total of 17 4in (102mm) guns as secondary armament including five triple mountings unique to this class of warship but for use against surface craft rather than for defence against air attack. *Repulse* was refitted in 1934–6 and some of the triple 4in mountings were removed to make way for an aircraft hangar and catapult aft of the funnels. More single 4in AA were fitted, together with two multiple 2pdr mountings and additional HA directors. The ship was scheduled for a more extensive refit at the end of 1941, but in the meantime she was sent to the Far East and was lost to Japanese air attack, along with the battleship *Prince of Wales*, off Malaya on 10 December 1941. *Renown*, on the other hand, was given a much more extensive refit during 1936–9 in which new lightweight machinery was installed,

the existing secondary armament was removed and replaced by a battery of 20 4.5in (114mm) DP guns controlled by four HA/LA directors, and the superstructure was completely rebuilt along the lines of the modernised Queen Elizabeth class battleships. Unusually for a capital ship, she retained fixed torpedo tubes carried on the upper deck. During World War II she was updated with the addition of radar equipment and additional light AA guns, and in 1943 the aircraft and catapult were removed. In April 1940 she fought a spirited engagement with the German battlecruisers *Scharnhorst* and *Gneisenau* but, despite some accurate gunnery, the two enemy ships were able to pull away and the result was inconclusive. She subsequently saw action in the Mediterranean and returned to the Home Fleet in 1942–3 before going out to the Far East in 1944. Returning home, she was laid up before the end of hostilities and was subsequently scrapped in 1948.

HMS Renown *on completion of a modernisation refit in 1939. Secondary armament now consisted of 20 4.5in (114mm) DP guns.* (Wright & Logan Collection)

SPECIFICATION

Class: Renown (battlecruiser) Data *Renown* as modernised
Displacement: 32,000 tons (37,410 tons full load)
Length: 750ft (228.6m) pp, 794ft (242m) oa
Beam: 87ft (26.5m); 103ft (31.4m) over bulges
Draught: 31.5ft (9.6m) full load
Machinery: 42 boilers, 4 shafts, Brown-Curtiss turbines, 112,000shp
Speed: 29kt
Range: 9,000nm (16,677km)
Complement: 1,309
Protection: Main belt 9in (229mm), bulkheads 4in (102mm), main deck 2.5–5in (63–127mm). Turrets 11in (279mm) faces, 7in (178mm) sides. Barbettes 4–7in (102–178mm). External bulges.
Armament: Guns: 6 15in/138mm (3 × 2), 20 4.5in/114mm DP (10 × 2), 24 2pdr AA (3 × 8), 16 0.5in/13mm AA (4 × 4). Torpedoes: 8 18in (457mm) fixed tubes (4 × 2).
Aircraft: 4. One athwartships catapult.
Ships in Class: *Renown* (1916), *Repulse* (1916)

HMS Rodney with main armament trained to port. (Sydney Goodman Collection)

The Washington Naval Treaty allowed Britain to build two new battleships which were subsequently laid down at the end of 1922 and completed in 1927. They were the only British battleships to be armed with 16in (406mm) guns which were carried in three triple turrets all grouped together forward of the bridge superstructure, which in turn was set well aft. This unusual arrangement allowed a reduction in the extent of armour protection required which, together with the acceptance of machinery of reduced output, brought the standard displacement within the laid-down 35,000 tons. Although the main armament could not train aft, this did not prove to be any great tactical disadvantage in practice, although blast damage to the bridge could occur with the guns trained aft of the beam.

Both ships had an active war, mostly with the Home Fleet and in the Mediterranean, although HMS *Nelson* saw action with the East Indies Fleet in 1945. A more serious drawback was their speed of only 22kt which made it difficult for them to operate with the new generation of fast battleships coming into service at the start of World War II. It was the 16in guns of HMS *Rodney* that played a

significant role in the final destruction of the German battleship *Bismarck*, but this only occurred because she had previously been slowed down as a result of torpedo attacks by aircraft.

Both ships were constantly modified during the war. The original fixed underwater torpedo tubes were removed, as were all aircraft handling arrangements. AA armament was increased, and by 1945 comprised over 40 2pdr and/or 40mm (1.6in), and some 60 20mm (0.8in) guns.

Having survived hostilities, both were scrapped in the late 1940s. Despite their rather ungainly appearance and allowing for the limitation in speed, they had proved a successful design and the general layout was adopted by the French Navy in the design of the Dunkerque class battlecruisers and the Richelieu class battleships.

SPECIFICATION

Class: Nelson (battleship) Data *Nelson* 1939
Displacement: 33,950 tons (38,000 tons full load)
Length: 710ft (216.4mm) oa
Beam: 106ft (32.3mm)
Draught: 31.5ft (9.6m) full load
Machinery: 8 boilers, 2 shafts, Brown-Curtiss SR geared turbines, 45,000shp
Speed: 23kt
Range: 16,500nm (30,574km) at 12kt
Complement: 1,314
Protection: Main belt 14in (355mm), bulkheads 13in (330mm) or 9in (229mm), middle deck 6.25in (159mm) maximum. Turrets 16in (406mm) faces, 12in (305mm) sides, 9in (229mm) crowns, barbettes 15in (381mm) or 14in (355mm). Internal bulges.
Armament: Guns: 9 16 in/406mm (3 × 3), 12 6 in/152mm (6 × 2), 6 4.7 in/119mm AA (3 × 2), 32 2pdr AA (3 × 8 and 8 × 1), 16 0.5 in/13mm AA (4 × 4). Torpedoes: 2 24.5in/622mm (2 × 1) fixed torpedo tubes.
Aircraft: 1 (2 in *Rodney*)
Ships in Class: *Nelson* (1925), *Rodney* (1925)

A late wartime view of HMS Nelson. (Sydney Goodman Collection)

King George V

HMS **King George V.** *(Sydney Goodman Collection)*

Under the terms of the various naval treaties, it was not until 1937 that Britain was able to start laying down new battleships, and at that time battleships were limited to a displacement of 35,000 tons and an armament of 16in (406mm) guns. However, the British government was actively campaigning for the armament to be reduced to 14in (355mm) guns and consequently the new King George V class of five battleships was designed to mount 12 such guns in three quadruple turrets. In order to keep within the tonnage limitations, it proved necessary to reduce B turret to a twin mounting so that the final main armament was 10 14in guns. By 1938 the signatories of the London Naval Treaties had set battleship parameters at 45,000 tons and 16in guns, but it was then too late to make any significant changes to the British vessels whose construction was being hastened as the outbreak of war became inevitable.

Even so, the *King George V* did not commission until the end of 1940 and the second ship, *Prince of Wales*, was only handed over in March 1941 so that she was still working up when sent into action in company with the ill-fated HMS *Hood* against the German battleship *Bismarck* on 21 May. She was hit several times and withdrew after the *Hood* was sunk. By the end of the year she was deployed to the Far East but, together with the battlecruiser *Repulse*, was sunk off the Malayan coast by Japanese aircraft.

The last three ships of the class were all in service by the end of 1942 and together with the *King George V* played a major part in various naval operations including the invasions of Sicily and Italy, and various Arctic convoy actions. It was in one of the latter that one of the few examples of a major gun action between capital ships occurred when the *Duke of York* sank the German battlecruiser *Scharnhorst* on Boxing Day 1943. In 1945 both *King George V* and *Howe* were serving with the British Pacific fleet when hostilities ended in August of that year. All four vessels were eventually scrapped in the late 1950s.

Throughout the war, the King George V class were constantly updated, in particular the light AA armament was significantly boosted. In 1943 the

aircraft and catapult were removed and the resulting space was filled in by a new deckhouse structure above which the ship's boats were stowed. The former boatdeck was then utilised for additional AA guns and their directors. In 1940–1, the first two ships were fitted with UP projectors on B and Y turrets, but these were subsequently replaced by multiple 2pdr mountings.

In 1939, four Lion class battleships were laid down which were broadly similar to the *King George V* but would have been armed with nine 16in guns in three triple mountings. With the outbreak of war they were suspended and eventually cancelled so that resources could be concentrated on more immediate projects. Britain subsequently built only one more battleship, HMS *Vanguard*, which was not completed until 1946 and was a slight enlargement of the Lion class design but adapted to use existing 15in (381mm) gun mountings.

SPECIFICATION

Class: King George V (battleship) Data as designed
Displacement: 35,000 tons (40,000 tons full load)
Length: 700ft (213.4m) pp, 745ft (227.1m) oa
Beam: 103ft (31.4m)
Draught: 31.5ft (9.6m) full load
Machinery: 8 boilers, 4 shafts, Parsons SR geared turbines, 110,000shp
Speed: 29kt
Range: 6,300nm (11,673km) at 20kt
Complement: 1,612
Protection: Main belt 15in (381mm) (maximum), bulkheads 10–12in (254–305mm), main deck 5–6in (127–152mm). Turrets 13in (330mm) faces, 9in (229mm) sides, 7in (178mm) rear, 6in (152mm) crowns. Barbettes 11–13in (229–330mm). Internal bulges.
Armament: 10 14in/355mm (2 × 4, 1 × 2), 16 5.25in/133mm DP (8 × 2), 32 2pdr AA (4 × 8), 16 0.5in AA (4 × 4).
Aircraft: 3. Fixed athwartships catapult.
Ships in Class: *King George V* (1939), *Prince of Wales* (1939), *Duke of York* (1940), *Anson* (1940), *Howe* (1940).

USS **Texas** *(BB 35) in January 1945.* (US Navy Historical Branch)

*A*rkansas and *Wyoming* were the oldest battle-ships in the US fleet at the time of Pearl Harbor in 1941. Originally armed with 12 12in (305mm) guns, the *Wyoming* was demilitarised in 1932 and converted to a gunnery training ship with half the main armament removed. She continued in that role throughout the war and was scrapped in 1947. Following a major refit in 1925–6, *Arkansas* was retained in the active fleet but in 1942 underwent a further refit in which all of the casemate battery was removed and the AA armament augmented to 10 3in (76mm) AA, 24 40mm (1.6in) and 32 20mm (0.8in) AA guns. She then served in the Atlantic helping to protect the convoys, but her main battery was used to great effect in support of the Normandy landings. She was subsequently used in the same role in the assaults on Iwo Jima and

Okinawa. After the war she was expended as a target in the atomic bomb tests at Bikini Atoll in 1946.

The two New York class ships, completed in 1914, were similar to the preceding Wyomings except that main armament was uprated to 10 14in (355mm) guns. In an apparently retrograde step, the new ships reverted to reciprocating machinery instead of steam turbines. Both *New York* and *Texas* were modified along the same lines as the *Arkansas* during World War II. Both served in the Atlantic, covering the North Africa landings in late 1942 and the Normandy landings in 1944 before being sent to the Pacific for operations against Iwo Jima and Okinawa, where *New York* was slightly damaged by a kamikaze attack. She, too, was expended as a target post-war, but *Texas* lives on today, preserved as a memorial at Galveston.

USS **New York** *(BB 34) in 1945. Note extensive radar arrays on the foremast.* (US Navy Historical Branch)

SPECIFICATION

Class: New York (battleship) Data *Texas* 1944
Displacement: 27,000 tons (32,000 tons full load)
Length: 565ft (172.2m) wl, 573ft (174.6m) oa
Beam: 95ft (29m); 106ft (32.3m) over bulges
Draught: 31.5ft (9.6m) full load
Machinery: 6 boilers, VTE reciprocating machinery, 2 shafts, 28,100ihp
Speed: 21kt
Range: 8,000nm (14,815km) at 11kt
Complement: 1,530
Protection: Main belt 6–12in (152–305mm), bulkheads 10in (254mm), main deck 2.5in (63mm) (max), lower deck 3.5in (89mm) (max). Turrets 8–14in (203–355mm). Barbettes 12in (305mm). External bulges.
Armament: 10 14in/355mm (5 × 2), 6 5in/127mm (6 × 1), 10 3in/76mm AA (10 × 1), 40 40mm/1.6in AA (10 × 4), 40 20mm/0.8in AA (40 × 1)
Aircraft: 3. Catapult mounted on Q turret amidships.
Ships in Class: *Texas* (1912), *New York* (1912)

Nevada

USS Nevada *(BB 36) in drydock at Pearl Harbor in 1935.* (US Navy Historical Branch)

Completed in 1916, these two battleships were armoured on the all-or-nothing principle in which the vital parts of the ship (turrets, barbettes, magazines and machinery) were heavily armoured while the rest of the ship was left virtually unprotected. In order to keep down the weight of armour, it was necessary to concentrate the main armament so that this class still mounted 10 14in (355mm) guns but the introduction of triple mountings in A and Y turrets reduced the total number of turrets to four. Compared to the previous flush-decked designs, the Nevadas had a forecastle deck extended aft almost as far as the mainmast. In service, the casemate-mounted secondary armament was found to be unworkable in rough weather and during refits in the 1920s both ships had these guns raised one deck. The typical lattice cage mast was replaced by tripods and aircraft catapults were installed atop X turret and on the stern. External bulges were also added.

In this guise, both ships were present at Pearl Harbor on the fateful 7 December 1941 and *Oklahoma* capsized after being torpedoed. *Nevada* was also badly hit but managed to get underway and was successfully beached to prevent her sinking. *Oklahoma* was later raised but was too badly damaged to be worth rebuilding. On the other hand, *Nevada* underwent a major refit in which a new taller superstructure was added, all the casemate guns were removed and a new battery of 16 5in (127mm) DP guns in eight twin turrets was added. A prominent recognition feature was a tall funnel cap raked aft to keep fumes away from the new higher bridge. She sub-

sequently spent the next two years with the Atlantic fleet and was part of the force covering the North Africa landings in November 1942. At the end of 1944 she redeployed to the Pacific in time to take part in the Iwo Jima and Okinawa landing operations. After the war she was a target ship for A-bomb tests and was finally scuttled off Hawaii in 1948.

SPECIFICATION

Class: Nevada (battleship) Data *Oklahoma* 1940
Displacement: 29,000 tons (34,000 tons full load)
Length: 575ft (175.3m) wl, 583ft (177.7m) oa
Beam: 95.25ft (29m); 108ft (32.9m) over bulges
Draught: 32ft (9.7m) full load
Machinery: *Oklahoma*: 6 boilers, VTE reciprocating machinery, 2 shafts, 24,800ihp. *Nevada*: geared turbines, 26,500shp.
Speed: 20.5kt
Range: 10,000nm (18,520km) at 11kt
Complement: c. 2,000
Protection: Main belt 8–13.5in (203–343mm), bulkheads 13.5in (343mm), decks 1.5–3in (38–76mm). Turrets 16–18in (406–457mm) faces, 10in (254mm) sides, 9in (229mm) rears, 5in (127mm) crowns. Barbettes 13.5in (343mm) (above decks). External bulges.
Armament: 10 14in/355mm (2 × 3, 2 × 2), 12 5in/51 127mm (12 × 1), 8 5in/25 127mm AA (8 × 1).
Aircraft: 3. Two catapults – stern and atop X turret.
Ships in Class: *Oklahoma* (1914), *Nevada* (1914)

Pennsylvania

A dramatic view of USS Pennsylvania (BB 38) carrying out a bombardment during operations to capture Guam, July 1944. The tremendous firepower of battleships made them ideally suited for this role. (US Navy Historical Branch)

The next two US battleships were developments of the Nevada class in which the main armament was increased to 12 14in (355mm) guns, all mounted in triple turrets. Underwater and internal protection was improved, but these and other changes resulted in an increase of standard displacement by some 4,000 tons. Both ships completed in 1916 and between 1928 and 1931 they were modernised along the lines of the Nevada class with cage masts replaced by tripod structures, a stern-mounted aircraft catapult, and revisions to the disposition of the secondary armament.

Both were present at Pearl Harbor and *Arizona* suffered a magazine explosion after being hit by torpedoes and bombs. She rolled over and sank with a heavy loss of life and was not subsequently raised. Today, the remains of her submerged hull are still visible and act as a memorial to all who lost their lives on 7 December 1941. *Pennsylvania* was in drydock at the time of the attack and was heavily damaged but was quickly repaired. At the end of 1942 she was taken in hand for a major refit in which the existing secondary armament was removed and replaced by a standard battery of 16 5in/38cal (127mm) DP guns in eight twin mountings carried high up at boat deck level where they commanded a good field of fire. In addition, 40 40mm (1.6in) and 50 20mm (0.8in) guns were added. The after tripod was removed and replaced with a large deckhouse carrying light AA guns and radar equipment. She spent the remain-

der of the war supporting Pacific operations but was badly damaged in an airborne torpedo attack in August 1945. She subsequently ended her days as a target ship, and was scuttled in 1948.

SPECIFICATION

Class: Pennsylvania (battleship) Data *Pennsylvania* 1943
Displacement: 33,100 tons (36,500 tons full load)
Length: 600ft (182.9m) wl, 608ft (185.3m) oa
Beam: 97ft (29.6m); 106.25ft (32.4m) over bulges
Draught: 33ft (10m) full load
Machinery: 6 boilers, geared turbines, 4 shafts, 31,500shp
Speed: 21kt
Range: 8,000nm (14.815km) at 12kt
Complement: 2,290
Protection: Main belt 8–14in (203–355mm), bulkheads 14in (355mm), decks 2–4in (51–102mm), funnel and boiler uptakes 9–15in (229–381mm). Turrets 18in (457mm) faces, 10in (254mm) sides, 9in (229mm) rear, 5in (127mm) crowns. Barbettes 14in (355mm). External bulges.
Armament: 12 14in/355mm (4 x 3), 16 5in/38 127mm DP (8 x 2), 40 40mm/1.6in AA (10 x 4), 50 20mm/0.8in AA (50 x 1).
Aircraft: 3. One stern catapult.
Ships in Class: *Pennsylvania* (1915), *Arizona* (1915)

New Mexico/Tennessee

USS Idaho (BB 42) carries out a bombardment of Okinawa, April 1945. (US Navy Historical Branch)

The New Mexico class, commissioned in 1917–19, were similar to the preceding Pennsylvania class except that the secondary armament was carried a deck higher and a distinctive clipper bow provided a useful recognition feature. Unusually, three ships were ordered instead of the usual pair, the additional funding coming from the sale of two older battleships to the Greek government. All three were modernised between 1930 and 1934 when the machinery was replaced (*New Mexico* initially had a turbo electric system), the cage lattice masts were replaced by more conventional tripods, some of the casemate 5in (127mm) guns were removed and the AA armament strengthened. Catapults were fitted on the stern and above X turret and external bulges were fitted. All three battleships were absent from Pearl Harbor and as the naval yards were fully occupied with rebuilding the damaged ships, the New Mexico class did not undergo any major reconstruction. Wartime modifications included the removal of the casemate 5in guns, further strengthening of the AA armament and the removal of the X turret catapult. Various radars were also fitted. Uniquely, the *Idaho* was eventually given a secondary armament of 10 5in/38 DP guns in single enclosed mountings. All three served in the Pacific although *New Mexico* and *Mississippi* were both damaged by kamikaze attacks in 1945. After the war *Mississippi* served for a while as a training and guided missile trials ship.

The two Tennessee class battleships were basically repeats of the New Mexico class except that they originally had two slim funnels and adopted turbo electric machinery. The hull was flush-sided as they were designed from the start to carry the secondary armament at upper deck level. At the time of Pearl Harbor they had been little modified and still retained the lattice masts. Both were badly damaged, and although patched up in the immediate aftermath of the attack, by late 1942 both began major reconstructions which took until 1944 in the case of the more seriously damaged *California*, although *Tennessee* recommissioned in May 1943. As rebuilt, the appearance of these ships was completely altered. Deep bulges increased beam to 114ft (34.7m) and displacement rose to 37,000 tons. A single funnel replaced the previous two slim stacks and an entirely new superstructure, closely resembling that of the more modern South Dakota class, was built. Secondary armament comprised a standard battery of 16 5in/38 DP guns backed up by almost 100 light AA guns. Supporting amphibious operations in the Pacific in 1944 and 1945, both ships were again damaged at varying times by shore artillery and kamikaze attacks. Laid up after the war, they were scrapped in 1959–60.

SPECIFICATION

Class: New Mexico/Tennessee (battleship) Data *New Mexico* 1940
Displacement: 33,400 tons (36,000 tons full load)
Length: 600ft (182.9m) wl, 624ft (190.2m) oa
Beam: 97.5ft (29.7m); 106.25ft (32.4m) over bulges
Draught: 34ft (10.4m) full load
Machinery: 4 (6 in *Mississippi* and *Idaho*) boilers, geared turbines, 4 shafts, 40,000shp
Speed: 21.5kt
Range: 9,000nm (16,677km) at 12kt
Complement: 1,930
Protection: Main belt 8–14in (203–355mm), bulkheads 14in (355mm), uptakes and funnel 9–16in (229–406mm), decks 4–6in (102–152mm). Turrets 9–18in (229–457mm). Barbettes 14in (355mm). External bulges.
Armament: 12 14in/355mm (4 × 3), 12 5in/51 (127mm) (12 × 1), 8 5in/25 (127mm) AA (8 × 1), 12 1.1in/28mm AA (3 × 4)
Aircraft: 3. Two catapults.
Ships in Class: New Mexico, Mississippi, Idaho (1917; Tennessee, California (1919)

Following severe damage at Pearl Harbor in 1941, USS Tennessee (BB 43) was substantially rebuilt and her profile completely altered. (US Navy Historical Branch)

UNITED STATES
Colorado

The battleship USS Maryland *(BB 46) fights desperately to stay afloat during the attack on Pearl Harbor. Alongside her is the hull of the capsized* Oklahoma. *(US Navy Historical Branch)*

The Colorado class were the last of the World War I era battleships to commission with the US Navy, although they were not completed until 1921–3. Four ships were originally ordered but under the terms of the Washington Treaty only three could be completed. The incomplete USS *Washington* was therefore used as a target for bombing trials and sunk in November 1924. Very similar to the preceding Tennessee class, the main difference was in the main armament which now comprised eight 16in (406mm) guns in four twin turrets. Turbo electric propulsion was again selected. As with other battleships, they were modified in the late 1920s by addition of aircraft catapults on the stern and atop X turret, the removal of submerged torpedo tubes, and a strengthening of the AA armament.

At the time of Pearl Harbor, Colorado was being refitted in America and retained her lattice masts for much of the war, together with the casemate 5in (127 mm) guns. By 1945 she carried eight 5in AA in single mounts and around 80 light AA guns (40mm/1.6in and 20mm/0.8in). *Maryland* was

damaged at Pearl Harbor but was not greatly altered when the subsequent repairs were completed, although a further refit in 1945 included the addition of 16 5in/38 DP in twin mountings. *West Virginia* was hit by four torpedoes in the Pearl Harbor attack and sank on an even keel in shallow water. She was salvaged and completely rebuilt along the lines of the Tennessee class (new superstructure, single funnel, increased beam, completely new secondary armament) and consequently bore little resemblance to her sister ships. All three were deployed in support of Pacific operations and, although damaged in kamikaze attacks in 1944–5, survived the war. They were scrapped in 1959–60.

Maryland **was rebuilt after Pearl Harbor and saw considerable action. This view shows her in 1945 following repairs after being hit by a kamikaze in November 1944.** *(US Navy Historical Branch)*

SPECIFICATION

Class: Colorado (battleship) Data *Maryland* as reconstructed 1944–5
Displacement: 31,500 tons (39,100 tons full load)
Length: 600ft (182.9m) wl, 624ft (190.2m) oa
Beam: 97.5ft (29.7m); 108ft (32.9m) over bulges
Draught: 35ft (10.7m) full load
Machinery: 8 boilers, Curtiss geared turbines (28,900shp), electric motors (27,200shp), 4 shafts
Speed: 21kt
Range: 8,000nm (14,824km) at 12kt
Complement: c. 2,000
Protection: Main belt 8–16in (203–406mm), bulkheads 14in (355mm), uptakes 9–16in (229–406mm), decks 2.5–3.5in (63–89mm). Turrets 9–18in (229–457mm). Barbettes 16in (406mm) (max). External bulges.
Armament: 8 16 in/406mm (4 × 2), 16 5in/127mm DP (8 × 2), 40 40mm/1.6in (10 × 4), 36 20mm/0.8in AA (36 × 1)
Aircraft: 3. Stern catapult.
Ships in Class: *Maryland* (1920), *Colorado* (1921), *West Virginia* (1921)

USS North Carolina *(BB 55) in 1943 off Hawaii. (US Navy Historical Branch)*

These two ships were the first of the new-generation fast battleships built by the US Navy; they complied with the 35,000-ton treaty limits and were armed with nine 16in (406mm) guns in three triple turrets. The combination of this heavy armament, together with extensive armour protection, meant that speed was only 28kt, a little slower than most foreign contemporaries but not a serious drawback. They were powerful ships, flush-decked with a handsome profile. The US Navy was fortunate in the availability of the ubiquitous 5in/38cal (127mm) DP guns, and 20 of these were shipped in twin turrets amidships where they commanded good arcs of fire. Up to three aircraft could be carried and these, together with two catapults and a crane, were all placed on the stern, an arrangement repeated in all subsequent US bat-tleship construction. Completed in 1941, both *North Carolina* and *Washington* had their light AA armament continually increased and upgraded, the latter carrying no fewer than 96 40mm (1.6in) guns in 24 quadruple mountings by 1945.

Both saw extensive action in the Pacific, taking part in most of the major campaigns, although at one stage *Washington* spent a brief period with the British Home Fleet in support of Arctic convoys. She later covered herself in glory by sinking the Japanese battleship *Kirishama* in a night action during the Second Battle of Guadalcanal in November 1942. Despite her excellent war record, she was laid up in 1947 and subsequently scrapped in 1961. Her sister ship, *North Carolina*, was more fortunate and ended up as a war memorial and museum at Wilmington.

An aerial view of the USS Washington *(BB 56) showing the disposition of the main and secondary armament. Note the tall tower carrying the radar-equipped gunnery DCT. (US Navy Historical Branch)*

SPECIFICATION

Class: North Carolina (battleship) Data *Washington* as completed 1941
Displacement: 35,000 tons (45,370 tons full load)
Length: 704ft (214.6m) wl, 729ft (222.2m) oa
Beam: 108ft (32.9 m)
Draught: 35ft (10.7 m)
Machinery: 8 boilers, General Electric geared turbines, 4 shafts, 121,000shp
Speed: 28kt
Range: 10,500nm (19,450km) at 12kt
Complement: 2,339
Protection: Main belt 8–16in (203–406mm), bulkheads 16in (406mm), main deck 6in (152mm), lower deck 4in (102mm). Turrets 18in (457mm) (max). Barbettes 16in (406mm).
Armament: 9 16in/406mm (3 × 3), 20 5in/127mm DP (10 × 2), 16 1.1in/28mm AA (4 × 4), 12 0.5in/13mm AA (12 × 1)
Aircraft: 3. Two stern catapults.
Ships in Class: *North Carolina* (1940), *Washington* (1940)

17

USS South Dakota in 1942. Note the arrangement of the catapults on the stern. (US Navy Historical Branch)

Again built to the 35,000-ton treaty limits, these ships were similar to the North Carolina class except that the hull was shortened by 50ft (15.2 m) so that armour protection could be improved without increasing overall displacement. As a consequence the midships section was foreshortened and the single funnel was faired into the back of the bridge structure. *South Dakota* was completed in March 1942 but mounted only 16 5in (127mm) guns (eight twin mountings), although she was fitted to act as a fleet flagship. The remaining three all carried the designed secondary armament of 20 5in guns. The shorter hull meant that installed power had to be increased in order to maintain a speed of 28kt. The aircraft arrangements were again located on the stern and the light AA armament was steadily augmented through the war.

South Dakota was constantly in action in the Pacific. Damaged by air attack on two occasions,

she was hit by enemy gunfire in November 1942, sustaining many casualties, and was also involved in a number of accidents including striking an uncharted rock, colliding with a destroyer, and suffering an internal turret explosion in 1945. *Indiana*, completed in April 1942, spent most of her subsequent career in the Pacific and was one of the first US battleships to be hit by a kamikaze, off Saipan in June 1944. After the war she was decommissioned (1947) and was scrapped in 1963. *Massachusetts* and *Alabama* were also completed in 1942 and initially served in the Atlantic, the former sustaining some damage in a gunnery duel with the French battleship *Jean Bart* at Casablanca during the North Africa landings in November 1942. Both subsequently joined the Pacific fleet and were laid up in 1947. However, they escaped the breakers yard: *Alabama* is preserved as a state memorial at Mobile, *Massachusetts* on the Fall River.

A view from the quarterdeck of the USS Massachusetts (BB 59) during the action off Casablanca in November 1942. (US Navy Historical Branch)

SPECIFICATION

Class: South Dakota (battleship) Data *Indiana* as completed 1942
Displacement: 35,000 tons (44,370 tons full load)
Length: 666ft (203m) wl, 680ft (207.3m) oa
Beam: 108.25ft (33m)
Draught: 36ft (11m) full load
Machinery: 8 boilers, geared turbines, 4 shafts, 130,000shp
Speed: 28kt
Range: 12,000nm (22,236km) at 12kt
Complement: c. 2,300
Protection: Main belt 8–16in (203–406mm), bulkheads 16in (406mm), main deck 6in (152mm), lower deck 4in (102mm). Turrets 18in (457mm) (max). Barbettes 16in (406mm).
Armament: 9 16in/406mm (3 × 3), 20 5in/127mm DP (10 × 2), 56 40mm/1.6in AA (14 × 4), 40 20mm 20mm/0.8in AA (40 × 1).
Aircraft: 3. Two stern catapults.
Ships in Class: South Dakota (1941), Indiana (1941), Massachusetts (1941), Alabama (1942)

An aerial view of USS Iowa *(BB 61). The hull shape with its fine bow and broad midships section was often likened to a Coca-Cola bottle!* (Author's Collection)

A colour view of one of the 20mm (0.8in) AA guns on the foredeck of the USS Iowa. (US Navy Historical Branch)

These were the largest Allied battleships and were only surpassed in size by the Japanese Yamato class. Superficially they represented little advance on the preceding South Dakota class as they carried the same main and secondary armament despite displacement rising by approximately 10,000 tons. Much of this was accounted for by heavily increased protection, but they were also some 200ft (61m) longer and, with machinery output almost doubled, they were the fastest battleships ever built, capable of 33kt. Their much greater size allowed more deck space for light AA guns and this, together with their high speed, made them ideal escorts for the fast carrier task forces which ranged the Pacific Ocean from 1943 onwards. The effectiveness of the light AA armament was increased by the provision of a radar-equipped director for each quadruple 40mm (1.6in) mounting. Their size also provided the space for command and communications staff so that they were almost invariably used as task force flagships.

All four entered service in 1943–4, the total construction time in some cases being fewer than three years – an excellent achievement for such

complex vessels. Two further vessels, *Illinois* and *Kentucky*, were cancelled although the machinery for the latter was eventually diverted to two fast combat support ships (*Sacramento* and *Camden*), which remain in service today with the US Navy. The four Iowa class battleships saw significant post-war service and were upgraded with modern weapon systems and cruise missiles, although all are now finally retired.

As a follow-on to the Iowa class, the US Navy projected five Montana class which would have been armed with 12 16in (406mm) guns on a displacement of 65,000 tons. Their construction was cancelled in 1943 when it was accepted that aircraft carriers were a more effective instrument of seapower.

USS Iowa *(BB 61). The mainmast attached to the after funnel is a post-war addition.* (Wright & Logan Collection)

A post-war view of USS Wisconsin *(BB 64) with one of her 16in (406mm) gun turrets trained to starboard.* (US Navy Historical Branch)

SPECIFICATION

Class: Iowa (battleship) Data *New Jersey* as completed 1943
Displacement: 45,000 tons (57,450 tons full load)
Length: 861ft (262.4m) wl, 887ft (270.4m) oa
Beam: 108ft (32.9m)
Draught: 36ft (11m) full load
Machinery: 8 boilers, geared turbines, 4 shafts, 212,000shp
Speed: 33kt
Range: 15,000nm (27,780km) at 12kt
Complement: 2,750–3,000
Protection: Main belt 8–16in (203–406mm), bulkheads 16in (406mm), main deck 6in (152mm), lower deck 4in (102mm). Turrets 18in (457mm) (max). Barbettes 16in (406mm).
Armament: 9 16in/406mm (3 × 3), 20 5in/127mm DP (10 × 2), 64 40mm/1.6in AA (16 × 4), 60 20mm/0.8in AA (60 × 1).
Aircraft: 3. Two stern catapults.
Ships in Class: *Iowa* (1942), *New Jersey* (1942), *Wisconsin* (1943), *Missouri* (1944)

Distant view of the USS Alaska *showing her camouflage scheme in colour. (US Navy Historical Branch)*

The US Navy never built conventional battle-cruisers and this pair of 27,000-ton warships armed with 12in (305mm) guns were officially classed as large cruisers. Nevertheless, their size, speed and armament would have ranked them as battlecruisers in any other navy. They owed their inception to reports that Japan was building battlecruisers similar to the German Deutschland and Scharnhorst classes, but these were actually unfounded. By the time the first two Alaska class were completed their role was determined as escorting the fast carriers, for which they were eminently suitable by virtue of their heavy AA armament and high speed (33kt). A third ship, *Hawaii*, was

launched in 1945, but construction was suspended in 1947. At one time it was planned to complete her as a guided missile ship but this was not implemented and she was finally scrapped in 1960. *Alaska* and *Guam* were completed in 1944 in time to participate in the final actions in the Pacific. They were laid up in 1947 and scrapped in 1960–1. Three further projected vessels of this class (*Philippines*, *Puerto Rico* and *Samoa*) were all cancelled in 1943.

SPECIFICATION

Class: Alaska (battlecruiser) Data *Alaska* as completed
Displacement: 27,500 tons (34,250 tons full load)
Length: 791ft (241.1m) wl, 808.5ft (246.4m) oa
Beam: 91ft (27.7m)
Draught: 32ft (9.7m) full load
Machinery: 8 boilers, geared turbines, 4 shafts, 150,000shp
Speed: 33kt
Range: 12,000nm (22,220km) at 15kt
Complement: 2,250
Protection: Main belt 5–9in (127–229mm), bulkheads 9in (229mm), decks 2–4.5in (51–114mm). Turrets 12.75in (324mm) faces, 5in (127mm), sides, rear, crown,. Barbettes 9in (229mm).
Armament: 9 12in/305mm (3 × 3), 12 5in/127mm DP (6 × 2), 56 40mm/1.6in AA (14 × 4), 34 20mm/0.8in (34 × 1)
Aircraft: 4 . Two catapults.
Ships in Class: *Alaska* (1943), *Guam* (1943)

USS Alaska photographed in November 1944. (US Navy Historical Branch)

Dunkerque in 1937. These imposing ships were designed to counter the German pocket battleships. (Wright & Logan Collection)

Laid down in 1932, the *Dunkerque* was the first of the new generation of fast battleships to be laid down by any navy prior to World War II. While the British and American navies were prevented from starting new construction until 1937, France (and Italy) did not regard herself as subject to this restriction and laid down a second ship (*Strasbourg*) in 1934. The layout of these ships with the main armament concentrated forward was obviously heavily influenced by the British Nelson class. Unusually, the eight 13in (330mm) guns were mounted in two quadruple turrets but these contributed to a more balanced profile than the British ships with their three triple turrets. A dual purpose battery of 5.1in (130mm) guns was grouped mostly aft while the aircraft handling arrangements were particularly well laid out. A hangar opened on to the quarterdeck which was equipped with a catapult and crane. The relatively light calibre of the main armament guns, coupled with a speed of almost 30 kt often led to these ships being referred to as battlecruisers, although French sources always referred to them as battleships.

As with most French ships, their wartime career was varied and short. At the start of hostilities they often co-operated with British forces in the search for German commerce raiders such as the *Graf Spee*, some of the few vessels that could catch and destroy them. However, when France fell in June 1940 they were both at Oran when the pre-emptive attack was launched by the Royal Navy. *Dunkerque* was heavily damaged and sank, although she was later refloated and taken to Toulon in 1942 where she was blown up in drydock on 27 November. *Strasbourg* made a spirited escape from Oran and fought off determined British attacks before reaching Toulon, and then acted as flagship of the Vichy fleet until November 1942 when she was scuttled. Although later raised, she was again sunk, by American air attack, in 1944, and after the war the hulk was raised and scrapped.

Model of the foredeck of Dunkerque showing the two quadruple 13in (330mm) gun turrets. (Author's Collection)

SPECIFICATION

Class: Dunkerque (battleship) Data as completed
Displacement: 26,500 tons (33,000 tons full load)
Length: 686ft (209.1m) pp, 704ft (214.6m) oa
Beam: 102ft (31.1m)
Draught: 31.5ft (9.6m) full load
Machinery: 6 boilers, 4 shafts, Parsons SR geared turbines, 112,500shp
Speed: 29.5kt
Range: 7,500nm (13.890km) at 15kt
Complement: 1,431
Protection: Main belt 5.75–9.75in (146–248mm), bulkheads 4–9in (102–229mm), main deck 5in (127mm). Turrets 13in (330mm) faces, 10in (254mm) sides, 6in (152mm) crowns. Internal anti-torpedo bulkheads.
Armament: 8 13in/330mm (2 × 4), 16 5.1in/130mm DP (3 × 4, 2 × 2), 8 37mm/1.5in AA (4 × 2), 32 13.2mm/0.5in AA (8 × 4).
Aircraft: 4. Stern-mounted catapult.
Ships in Class: Dunkerque (1935), Strasbourg (1936)

Richelieu

The French battleship Richelieu *after a refit in the United States. (Sydney Goodman Collection)*

The basic design of the preceding Dunkerque class formed the basis for the Richelieu class battleships of which the first was laid down in 1935. Displacement rose to a nominal 35,000 tons, a heavier main armament of 15in (381mm) guns was mounted, and armour protection was considerably increased.

The name ship, *Richelieu,* had a particularly varied career, probably unmatched by any other capital ship. Virtually complete at the time of the German invasion of France in June 1940, she managed to sail to Dakar on the Atlantic coast of French West Africa and was then in action against British and Free French forces making an abortive attempt to capture the port in July. The accurate fire from her 15in guns was instrumental in persuading the attackers to withdraw, although she was damaged by a torpedo hit from a British aircraft. In 1943, following the collapse of the Vichy government, the *Richelieu* transferred to the Allied cause and sailed for the United States where she underwent a major refit. The hangar and aircraft arrangements were removed and the light AA armament augmented to include 57 40mm (1.6in) and 50 20mm (0.8in) guns. In 1944 she joined the British Far Eastern Fleet and saw action against Japanese forces before returning to France at the end of the war. She had a long peacetime career and did not decommission until 1959.

The second ship, *Jean Bart,* was incomplete at the time of the German invasion but managed to get away from St Nazaire with only half the machinery in working order and only one 15in gun turret fitted. She was taken to Casablanca where she remained throughout the war, being severely damaged during the Torch landings of November 1942. She returned to France after the war and was finally completed in 1949.

A third ship, *Clemenceau*, was laid down in 1939 but the incomplete hull was eventually destroyed in 1944. A fourth vessel, *Gascogne*, was also projected but was never laid down. Interestingly, the layout of the ship was to have been altered with a single quadruple turret fore and aft to give a more balanced layout.

SPECIFICATION

Class: Richelieu (battleship) Data *Richelieu* as designed
Displacement: 35,000 tons (47,500 tons full load)
Length: 794ft (242m) pp, 813ft (247.8m) oa
Beam: 108ft (32.9m)
Draught: 31.75ft (9.7m) full load
Machinery: 6 boilers, 4 shafts, Parsons SR geared turbines, 150,000shp
Speed: 30kt
Range: 10,000nm (18,520km) at 12kt
Complement: 1,550
Protection: Main belt 13.6in (345mm), bulkheads 9–15in (229–381mm), main deck 6.75in (171mm). Turrets 17.5in (445mm) faces, 10.6in (270mm) sides, 7.75in (197mm) crowns.
Armament: 8 15in/381mm (2 × 4), 9 6in/152mm DP (3 × 3), 12 3.9in (99mm) AA (6 × 2), 16 37mm/1.5in AA (8 × 2), 8 13.2mm/10.5in AA (2 × 4)
Aircraft: 3. Two stern catapults.
Ships in Class: Richelieu (1939), Jean Bart (1940), Clemenceau (not completed)

Close-up view of a model showing the bridge and one of the quadruple 15in (381mm) gun turrets aboard the Richelieu. *Note the many light AA guns. (Author's Collection)*

Pre-war view of the Admiral Graf Spee. Note the tall bridge structure and the seaplane on a catapult abaft the funnel. (Author's Collection)

Under the terms of the 1919 Treaty of Versailles, Germany was only permitted to build battleships with a maximum displacement of 10,000 tons armed with 11in (279mm) guns. It was envisaged that the resulting ships would be similar to the obsolete pre-dreadnoughts and would not pose any threat to the much larger capital ships of the British and French navies. However, by utilising modern welded construction, dispensing with thick armour plating, and concentrating the main armament in two triple turrets, the design was nominally kept within the tonnage limit. The adoption of diesel machinery gave these ships a very long range and a turn of speed faster than contemporary battleships. Consequently, with the exception of the British battlecruisers, they could outrun anything they did not outgun and caused a considerable stir in naval circles. They were also difficult to classify. The official German designation was *Panzerschiffe* (armoured ship), although they were popularly known as pocket battleships. Their obvious mission was to attack Allied merchant ships across the world's trade routes and, certainly in the early part of the war, they tied down enormous Allied resources.

The first to enter service, in 1933 was the *Deutschland*, although she was renamed *Lützow* in 1940. The remaining pair were completed in 1934–6 and differed in some details. The bridge was taller and better arranged, beam was increased by 3ft (1m) and the aircraft and catapult were re-sited abaft the funnel. All three carried their torpedo tubes in armoured housings on the stern. The *Graf Spee* was famously outmanoeuvred by British cruisers in the battle of the River Plate and was subsequently scuttled on 17 December 1939. In 1940–1 the *Admiral Scheer* had a highly successful career as a commerce raider in the Atlantic and Indian oceans and was later deployed in Norwegian waters. She almost survived the war but was sunk by bombs while in dock at Kiel on 9 April 1945. The *Lützow* made only one commerce raiding sortie and spent the rest of the war in northern European waters. Torpedoed twice, she was also fatally hit by RAF bombers in March/April 1945 although the damaged hull was towed to Russia after the war.

The midships section of the Deutschland (later renamed Lützow) showing the bridge and rangefinders. Note the single 5.9in guns and an He.60 floatplane on the catapult. (Maritime Photo Library)

SPECIFICATION

Class: Deutschland (armoured ship) Data *Deutschland* as completed
Displacement: 11,700 tons (15,900 tons full load)
Length: 593ft (180.7m) pp, 616ft (187.8m) oa
Beam: 68ft (20.7m)
Draught: 23ft (7m) full load
Machinery: 2 shafts, 8 MAN diesel motors (4 per shaft), 56,800bhp
Speed: 26kt
Range: 10,000nm (18,520km) at 19kt
Complement: 1,150
Protection: Main belt 3.25in (83mm) maximum, main deck 1.5in (38mm) (3in/76mm over magazines). Turrets 5.5in (140mm) faces, 4in (102mm) sides. Barbettes 4in (102mm). External bulges.
Armament: Guns: 6 11in/279mm (2 × 3), 8 5.9in/150mm (8 × 1), 6 4.1in/104mm AA (3 × 2), 8 37mm/1.5in AA, 10 20mm/0.8in AA. Torpedoes: 8 21in (533mm) tubes (2 × 4)
Aircraft: Two. One catapult.
Ships in Class: Deutschland/Lützow (1931), Admiral Scheer (1933), Admiral Graf Spee (1934)

Scharnhorst *follows her sister ship* Gneisenau *during Operation Juno, the invasion of Norway in 1940. (WZ Bilddienst)*

These two handsome ships redefined the battlecruiser concept by retaining heavy armour protection but reducing the weight of the main armament rather than the traditional concept of lightly armoured but heavily armed fast capital ships. As completed in 1938 and 1939, these ships featured a straight stem, but both were subsequently modified with raked clipper bows to improve seaworthiness in rough weather. The main armament of nine 11in (279mm) guns was adequate for most purposes but the secondary armament of 14 4.1in (104mm) guns controlled by four HA directors was one of the most effective of the period. During World War II modifications included the removal of the aircraft and catapults and the addition of several 20mm/0.8in AA guns.

In the early part of the war, these ships enjoyed considerable success, making two sorties into the Atlantic sinking many merchant ships and the armed merchant cruiser *Rawalpindi*. In the Norwegian campaign they intercepted and sank the British carrier *Glorious*. After their second Atlantic sortie they ended up at Brest and in a famous attempt to return home they sailed up the English Channel in February 1942, right under the noses of the British forces. However, the *Gneisenau* was seriously damaged by mines as she reached the North Sea and was later heavily damaged by bombing while undergoing repairs at Kiel so that she saw no further action. *Scharnhorst* was also mined in the same operation but was repaired and sent north to operate against British Arctic convoys. In one such action she was intercepted and sunk by the British battleship *Duke of York* on Boxing Day 1943.

SPECIFICATION

Class: Scharnhorst (battlecruiser) Data as completed
Displacement: 31,800 tons (38,900 tons full load)
Length: 741.5ft (226m) wl, 771ft (235m) oa
Beam: 100ft (30.5m)
Draught: 32ft (9.8m) full load
Machinery: 12 high-pressure boilers, Brown Boveri geared turbines, 3 shafts, 160,000shp
Speed: 32kt
Range: 10,000nm (18,520km) at 19kt
Complement: 1,800
Protection: Main belt 12–13in (305–330mm) amidships, 3–5in (76–127mm) ends, main deck 4.5in (114mm) maximum. Turrets 14.25in (362mm) faces, 9.75in (248mm) sides, 4in (102mm) rear. Barbettes 14in (355mm). Secondary turret 6in (152mm).
Armament: Guns: 9 11in/279mm (3 × 3), 12 5.9in/150mm (4 × 2 and 4 × 1), 14 4.1in/104mm AA (7 × 2), 16 37mm/1.5in AA (8 × 2). Torpedoes: 6 21in (533mm) tubes (2 × 3)
Aircraft: Four. Two catapults.
Ships in Class: *Scharnhorst* (1936), *Gneisenau* (1936)

Scharnhorst *was one of the most active German capital ships during World War II but was sunk by British forces on Boxing Day 1943. (WZ Bilddienst)*

Bismarck

Bismarck *running trials in the Baltic in 1940.* (WZ Bilddienst)

These were the largest German warships of World War II and among the most powerful battleships ever built. Although the main armament comprised only 15in (381mm) guns, they were very heavily armoured and their standard displacement of around 42,000 tons was well over the 35,000-ton limit most other navies nominally complied with. For some reason the German Navy failed to develop a good all-round medium-calibre DP gun and consequently these ships carried a secondary armament of 5.9in (150mm) guns to ward off destroyer attacks and a tertiary battery of 4.1in (104mm) guns for AA defence. Despite this the AA defence was extremely good, particularly as there were no fewer than six HA directors. German optical and electronic equipment was of the highest order, and this partially accounted for the German Navy's well-deserved reputation for accurate gunnery.

This was never more clearly demonstrated than on the *Bismarck*'s maiden voyage when she was intercepted by the *Hood* and *Prince of Wales* and sank the former with only her fifth salvo! Nevertheless, her fate was sealed and after a dramatic chase lasting several days she was eventually slowed down by aircraft torpedoes before being brought to bay by the British battleships *Rodney* and *King George V* on 27 May 1941.

Her sister ship *Tirpitz* was completed in 1941 and was based in Norway, thereafter posing a constant threat to British convoys and tying down substantial resources. She was finally sunk in Tromsø fjord by RAF Lancasters carrying 12,000lb (5,440kg) Tallboy bombs on 12 November 1944.

SPECIFICATION

Class: Bismarck (battleship) Data *Bismarck* 1940
Displacement: 41,700 tons (50,900 tons full load)
Length: 794ft (242m) wl, 823ft (250.9m) oa
Beam: 118ft (36m)
Draught: 33ft (10m) full load
Machinery: 12 boilers, Brown-Boveri geared turbines, 3 shafts, 138,000shp
Speed: 29kt
Range: 8,100nm at 19kt
Complement: 2,200
Protection: Main belt 12.75in (324mm) (max), decks 2–4.5in (51–114mm). Turrets 14in (355mm) face, 8.5in (216mm) sides, 5in (127mm) crown. Barbettes 13.5in (343mm).
Armament: Guns: 8 15in/381mm (4 × 2), 12 5.9in/150mm (6 × 2), 16 4.1in/104mm AA (8 × 2), 16 37mm/1.5in AA (8 × 2), 36 20mm/0.8in AA (4 × 4, 6 × 2, 8 × 1). Torpedoes: 8 21in (533mm) tubes (2 × 4) in *Tirpitz* only.
Aircraft: Six. Fixed athwartships catapult.
Ships in Class: *Bismarck* (1939), *Tirpitz* (1939)

The battleship *Tirpitz* **with her 15in guns trained to port.** (WZ Bilddienst)

Doria/Cavour

*Post-war view of the **Andrea Doria** at Malta. As modernised, the profile of these battleships was remarkably similar to the later Littorio class. (Wright & Logan Collection)*

These four battleships were all completed in 1914–16 and were originally armed with 13 12in (305 mm) guns in an unusual arrangement of a triple and twin turret forward and aft, and a third triple turret mounted amidships between the well-spaced tall funnels. They were built in two sub-groups with the second pair carrying a heavier secondary armament and having the midships turret lowered by one deck. In the late 1930s, all four were extensively modernised to such an extent that, apart from being 3kt slower, they were virtually the equal of the later Littorio class (cf). The whole conversion involved the lengthening of the hull by approximately 30ft (9m), new boilers and machinery in a twin shaft arrangement replaced the previous four shaft installation, the centre turret was removed and the calibre of the remaining guns increased from 12in to 12.6in (320mm), a new secondary battery was fitted together with modern fire control equipment, armour and protection was considerably enhanced, and an entirely new superstructure was erected. This process took almost four years for each ship. The Cavour class completed their modernisations in 1937, while the Doria class followed in 1940.

All four were present during the British attack on Taranto and *Cavour* sank in shallow water after a torpedo hit. Although raised, repairs were never completed and she saw no further service. *Cesare* and *Doria* were unscathed; *Duilio* suffered a torpedo hit but did not sink. *Cesare* survived the war and was passed to Russia as war reparations. The remaining pair were interned at Malta after the Italian surrender and served as training ships for a short period after the war before being scrapped in 1957–8.

SPECIFICATION

Class: Doria/Cavour classes (battleship) Data *Andrea Doria* 1940 as modernised
Displacement: 25,924 tons (29,000 tons full load)
Length: 597ft (182m) wl, 613ft (186.8m) oa
Beam: 92ft (28m)
Draught: 29ft (8.8m) full load
Machinery: 8 boilers, Belluzo geared turbines, 2 shafts, 85,000shp
Speed: 27kt
Range: 4,250nm (7,870km) at 12kt
Complement: 1,490
Protection: Main belt 5–9.75in (127–248mm), decks 1.5–3.5in (38–89mm). Turrets 11in (279mm) faces. Barbettes 11in (279mm).
Armament: 10 12.6in/320mm (2 × 3, 2 × 2), 12 5.3in/135mm (4 × 3), 10 3.5in/89mm AA (10 × 1), 19 37mm/1.5in AA, 12 20mm/0.8in AA.
Aircraft: None carried.
Ships in Class: Conte di Cavour (1911), Giulio Cesare (1911), Andrea Doria (1913), Caio Duilio (1913)

The Littorio *alongside at La Spezia. A row of 3.5in AA guns is visible and one of the triple 6in turrets can be seen on the left.* (WZ Bilddienst)

Like the French, the Italian Navy made an early start on the construction of modern fast battleships and two Littorio class were laid down in 1934, with a third following in 1938. With nine 15in (381mm) guns in three triple turrets and two closely spaced funnels, their profile was similar to the later US Washington class battleships. However, as with the German Navy, the Italians did not have a suitable dual-purpose gun available (although an excellent 5.23in (133mm) gun was later developed for the Capitani Romani class light cruisers) and consequently there was a secondary armament of 6in (152mm) guns and tertiary armament of 12 3.5in (89mm) AA guns arranged in batteries of six single turrets on either side amidships.

The *Littorio* had a hectic war and was hit by three torpedoes in the famous night attack on Taranto in November 1940. She was eventually repaired and put back into service but was again torpedoed in June 1942 while engaged in operations against Malta convoys. The following year she was damaged by air attack while in harbour at La Spezia and, following the Italian surrender, she was damaged by a German glider bomb while on passage to Malta. Interned for the rest of the war, she finally decommissioned in 1948. *Vittorio Veneto* escaped damage at Taranto but was hit by a torpedo during the Battle of Matapan. Later that year she was again torpedoed, this time by a British submarine, but in both cases she was able to return home for repairs. From 1943 she was interned and was subsequently laid up in 1948. Both vessels were scrapped in 1960. The third ship, *Roma*, was not completed until mid-1942 and saw no operational employment. While on passage to Malta on 9 September 1943 following the Italian surrender she was attacked and sunk by German glider bombs, the first example of a major warship being destroyed by a guided missile. A new era of naval warfare had dawned.

Vittorio Veneto *at speed in 1943.* (Robert Hunt Library)

SPECIFICATION

Class: Littorio (battleship) Data *Littorio* as completed 1940
Displacement: 41,377 tons (46,000 tons full load)
Length: 762ft (232.3m) wl, 780ft (237.7m) oa
Beam: 107ft (32.6m)
Draught: 32ft (9.8m) full load
Machinery: 8 boilers, Belluzo geared turbines, 4 shafts, 139,000shp
Speed: 30kt
Range: 4,580nm (8,840km) at 16kt
Complement: c. 1,900
Protection: Main belt 9–12in (229–305mm), decks 6in (152mm) (max). Turrets 13.5in (343mm) (max). Barbettes 13.5in (343mm). Pugilise system of internal anti-torpedo spaces.
Armament: 9 15in /381mm (3 × 3), 12 6in/152mm (4 × 3), 12 3.5in/89mm AA (12 × 1), 20 37mm/1.5in AA (10 × 2), 20 20mm/0.8in AA (10 × 2)
Aircraft: 3. One stern catapult.
Ships in Class: *Littorio* (1937), *Vittorio Veneto* (1937), *Roma* (1940)

A view of the battleship Kirishima *in the 1930s.* (US Navy Historical Branch)

These were the oldest Japanese battleships to see service in World War II and were designed as battlecruisers in Britain with the lead ship, *Kongo*, actually being built by Vickers Armstrong in their Barrow yard. The remaining pair were then built in Japan and all three were the first Japanese ships to mount 14in (355mm) guns. In the mid-1930s they underwent a substantial reconstruction which involved the lengthening of the hull by 25ft (7.6m), new boilers and machinery, funnels reduced from three to two, increased armour protection and external bulges fitted. A new tall bridge structure replaced the tripod foremast. In this guise they were redesignated as battleships, although under the terms of the First London Naval Treaty the *Hiei* was demilitarised by the removal of armour and guns. However, she was restored to fighting trim in a refit between 1936 and 1940, and all four ships subsequently saw arduous service despite their age.

Hiei and *Kirishima* were lost in night actions off Guadalcanal in November 1942, the latter to the gunfire of the US battleship *Washington*. The remaining pair had some of the 6in (152mm) guns removed to make room for up to 94 25mm (1in) AA guns and four additional 5in (127mm) guns. *Kongo* was torpedoed and sunk by a US submarine on 21 November 1944, while *Haruna* was first damaged in March 1945, and finally sunk on 28 July by air attacks from US carrier-based aircraft.

SPECIFICATION

Class: Kongo (battleship) Data *Kongo* 1940
Displacement: 31,720 tons (36,300 tons full load)
Length: 654ft (199m) pp, 728.5ft (222m) oa
Beam: 95ft (29m)
Draught: 32ft (9.8m) full load
Machinery: 8 boilers, Kanpon geared turbines, 4 shafts, 136,000shp
Speed: 30.5kt
Range: 10,000nm (18,520km) at 18kt
Complement: 1,437
Protection: Main belt 8in (203mm), deck 2.75in (70mm). Turrets 9in (229mm).
Armament: Guns: 8 14in/355mm (4 × 2), 14 6in/152mm (14 × 1), 8 5in/127mm AA (4 × 2), 20 25mm/1in AA (10 × 2)
Aircraft: 3. One catapult abaft X turret.
Ships in Class: Kongo, Hiei (1912); Kirishima, Haruna (1913)

Hiei **was used as a training ship in the 1930s with a reduced armament, as shown here. By 1940 she was modernised and rearmed for front-line service.** (US Navy Historical Branch)

Fuso/Ise

Battleship Ise *as converted to a hybrid aircraft carrier in 1943.*

A pre-war view of the Hyuga *as a conventional battleship.* (Maritime Photo Library)

The Yamashiro *in 1930.* (Maritime Photo Library)

The *Fuso* and *Yamashiro* were completed in the early part of World War I and carried a main armament of 12 14in (355mm) guns in six twin turrets, two forward, two aft and two amidships fore and aft of the second funnel. The succeeding *Ise* and *Hyuga* were slightly enlarged versions in which the midship guns were concentrated in a superfiring arrangement abaft the funnels. This permitted a more efficient use of internal space and gave more room for the machinery. Between 1930 and 1935 the first pair were modernised along now familiar lines with alterations to the hull, fitting of protective bulges, new machinery of increased output, and improvements to the armament. A catapult was fitted and provision made for up to three aircraft. The trademark pagoda bridge structure was erected, being particularly tall in these ships, and the boiler uptakes were trunked into a single funnel. Both *Fuso* and *Yamashiro* were lost to overwhelming Allied firepower on 25 October 1944 in the Battle of Surigao Strait.

The second pair, *Ise* and *Hyuga*, underwent a similar modernisation in 1936 but, following the heavy carrier losses at Midway in 1942, they were taken in hand for conversion to hybrid aircraft carriers. The after 14in turrets and superstructure were removed and a hangar and flight deck erected over the stern. Up to 22 seaplanes could be carried which were launched by catapults mounted on either beam just forward of the flight deck. On their return, the aircraft would alight on the sea and be retrieved by crane. This was a cumbersome method of operation at best, and by the time the conversions were completed in late 1943 the IJN was already beginning to suffer a shortage of pilots and aircraft. Consequently the catapults were eventually removed and the flight deck given over to light AA guns and a rather bizarre wire trailing rocket launcher system which proved completely ineffective. Both ships were bombed and sunk in Kure harbour in July 1945, where they had been laid up due to lack of fuel and aircraft.

SPECIFICATION

Class: Fuso/Ise (battleship) Data *Ise* 1937
Displacement: 35,800 tons (40,100 tons full load)
Length: 642ft (195.7m) pp, 708ft (215.8m) oa
Beam: 104ft (31.7m)
Draught: 30ft (9.1m) full load
Machinery: 8 boilers, Kanpon geared turbines, 4 shafts, 80,825shp
Speed: 25.25kt
Range: 9,500nm (17,603km) at 16kt
Complement: 1,376
Protection: Main belt 3–12in (76–305mm), decks 1.25–2.5in (32–64mm). Turrets 12in (305mm) faces, 8in (203mm) sides.
Armament: 12 14in/355mm (6 × 2), 16 5.5in/140mm (16 × 1), 8 5in/127mm AA (4 × 2), 20 25mm/1in AA (10 × 2)
Aircraft: One stern catapult.
Ships in Class: Fuso (1914), Yamashiro (1915), Ise (1916), Hyuga (1917)

Graphic image of the battleship Nagato *armed with eight 16in (406mm) guns.*

Battleship Mutsu *in 1933 prior to a modernisation in which the distinctive fore funnel was removed.* (Maritime Photo Library)

These two ships were intended to be part of a class of eight ships and embodied much experience gained during World War I. The remaining six ships were cancelled, but when completed in 1920 the *Nagato* and *Mutsu* were the first battleships in the world to be armed with 16in (406mm) guns, although the US Colorado class were completed shortly afterwards and the British were permitted to build two new 16in gun battleships to maintain the status quo. The two Japanese ships were modernised in 1934–6 when protection was improved by the addition of bulges and a triple bottom, elevation of the main armament guns was increased, new lightweight machinery was fitted which resulted in the previous two funnels being replaced by one tall funnel amidships, and a new massive pagoda bridge structure was added.

Mutsu was lost due to an internal magazine explosion in June 1943 while at anchor in Hiroshima bay which destroyed the ship and killed 1,222 of her crew. During the war *Nagato* was fitted with radar, a Type No. 21 atop the pagoda bridge structure and a Type No. 13 air warning radar at the mainmast. She was seriously damaged by air attack off Samar in October 1944 and saw no further action. Surrendered to US forces at the end of the war, she was expended as a target during the Bikini Atoll A-bomb tests in 1946.

SPECIFICATION

Class: Nagato (battleship) Data *Nagato* 1944
Displacement: 39,130 tons (46,350 tons full load)
Length: 699ft (213m) pp, 725ft (221m) wl, 734ft (223.7m) oa
Beam: 113.5ft (34.6m)
Draught: 31ft (9.4m) full load
Machinery: 10 boilers, Kanpon geared turbines, 4 shafts, 82,300shp
Speed: 25kt
Range: 8,650nm (16,028km) at 16kt
Complement: 1,368
Protection: Main belt 4–13in (102–330mm), decks 4.5in (114mm) (max). Turrets 14in (355mm) faces. External bulges.
Armament: 8 16in/406mm (4 × 2), 16 5.5in/140mm (16 × 1), 8 5in/127mm AA (4 × 2), 98 25mm/1in AA
Aircraft: 3. One catapult abaft mainmast, offset to port.
Ships in Class: Nagato (1919), Mutsu (1920)

A distant view of Musashi *leaving Brunei in October 1944 on her way to participate in the Leyte Gulf battles where she was sunk by US naval aircraft.* (US Navy Historical Branch)

These monsters were, by a substantial margin, the largest battleships ever built and, at 64,000 tons, were nearly twice the displacement of most Allied battleships. Their massive 18in (457mm) guns also outranged any Allied warship and they were heavily armoured. The Japanese thinking was that such material superiority could help overcome the numerical advantage in capital ships held by the American Navy. In practice, by the time they were completed in 1941-2, the day of the battleship was almost over and both the *Yamato* and *Musashi* were sunk by air attack from US Navy carrier-based aircraft. In fact, as the major surface warships of the IJN, they saw relatively little action and were preserved as a fleet, taking part only in important operations such as Midway (*Yamato* only), Philippine Sea and Leyte Gulf. *Musashi* was lost in the latter campaign while *Yamato* was sacrificed in a last desperate sortie from Japan on 7 April 1945, almost 2,500 of her crew going down with her. A third ship, *Shinano*, was completed as the world's largest aircraft carrier in November 1944. Intended to oper-

View of the battleship Yamato *showing the massive 18in (457mm) gun turrets and emphasising the great beam of these ships.*

ate as a support carrier, her career was distressingly brief and she was sunk by the US submarine *Archerfish* on her maiden voyage on 29 November 1944.

Fascinating graphic showing the midships section of the battleship Musashi *with its formidable array of 5in (127mm) and 25mm (1in) AA guns.*

SPECIFICATION

Class: Yamato (battleship) Data *Yamato* as completed 1941

Displacement: 64,170 tons (71,660 tons full load)

Length: 800.5ft (244m) pp, 840ft (256m) wl, 863ft (263m) oa

Beam: 127.75ft (38.9m)

Draught: 35.5ft (10.8m) (mean)

Machinery: 12 boilers, Kanpon geared turbines, 4 shafts, 150,000shp

Speed: 27.5kt

Range: 7,200nm (13,330km) at 16kt

Complement: c. 2,500

Protection: Main belt 16in (406mm), decks 7.75in (197mm). Turrets 20–25.5in (508–648mm).

Armament: 9 18in/457mm (3 × 3), 12 6.1in/155mm DP (6 × 2), 12 5in/127mm AA (6 × 2), 24 25mm/1in (8 × 3), 4 13mm/0.5in MG (2 × 2)

Aircraft: 6. Two stern catapults.

Ships in Class: *Yamato, Musashi* (1940); *Shinano* (1944)

AIRCRAFT CARRIERS

The concept of a large warship equipped with a full-length flight deck and capable of supporting operations by conventional fixed-wing aircraft evolved during World War I, although it was not until the mid-1920s that the first purpose-designed aircraft carriers were completed. The British Royal Navy was the leader in this field. By 1918 it had already commissioned HMS *Argus*, converted from a liner and the first carrier with a full-length flight deck. By 1930 there was also HMS *Hermes*, the world's first purpose-designed carrier, HMS *Eagle* (converted from a battleship originally destined for Chile), and three more large carriers converted from World War I battlecruisers. Experience gained with these vessels led to the 22,000-ton *Ark Royal* being launched in 1937, perhaps the most advanced aircraft carrier of its time. By the outbreak of war in 1939, the 24,000-ton Illustrious class were under construction, a major feature of these ships being an innovative armoured deck which proved its worth time and time again during World War II.

Unfortunately for the Royal Navy, its initial advantage in carrier numbers and design was almost totally negated by the fact that it had relinquished control of its air arm to the fledgling Royal Air Force in 1918, which was then responsible for the provision and operation of naval aircraft until the Admiralty eventually regained control in 1939. The result of this unfortunate arrangement was that the performance and quality of British naval aircraft fell substantially behind that of other navies, particularly those of America and Japan. Even having regained control, the Admiralty lacked the necessary expertise and experience to specify and produce first-class naval aircraft and, with the possible exception of the Fairey Firefly strike fighter, was eventually dependent on the supply of US naval aircraft types such as the Hellcat, Corsair and Avenger in order to build up credible carrier air groups for the final stages of the war in the Pacific.

As with battleships and other capital ships, the building of aircraft carriers in the inter-war years was subject to various treaty limitations. The 1921 Washington agreement limited them to a displacement of 27,000 tons and the maximum gun armament at 8in (203mm) calibre. It also specified that they could only be replaced when 20 years old, although carriers in existence at that time were not included and could be replaced at any time. The maximum total carrier tonnage allowed to the US and Britain was 135,000 tons with proportionate reductions for the other navies. Vessels under 10,000 tons were not included in this total. The 1930 London Treaty subsequently laid down the odd provision that carriers could not be less than 10,000 tons, and the 1935 London Treaty reduced maximum displacement to 22,000 tons, mainly at the insistence of Britain.

As already related, Britain started with a significant advantage in carrier numbers and for a while the United States was content with the two converted battlecruisers, *Lexington* and *Saratoga*. A further carrier, and the first US vessel to be designed as such, was not laid down until 1931. Construction of *Yorktown* and *Enterprise* left only 15,000 tons available for a further carrier which resulted in the *Wasp*, completed in 1940. With the expiration of treaty limits a third Yorktown class was laid down before wartime construction standardised on the magnificent Essex class. Unfettered by interservice rivalry, the US Navy was able to concentrate on the development of first-rate aircraft and effective tactics so that they subsequently set the standard which the Royal Navy struggled to attain throughout the war. That is not to say that the British did not contribute. In particular, the introduction of radar-assisted control of fighters in defence of a task force was pioneered by the Royal Navy in the fierce Malta convoy battles of 1941 and 1942, and this hard-won experience was eagerly adopted by the US Navy.

The only other significant carrier power was the Imperial Japanese Navy which, like the Americans, was quick to realise the potential of carrier-based aviation. By 1941 their air groups were probably the best trained and armed in the world, although this came as a great surprise to the Allies. Their strike at Pearl Harbor was modelled on the success of the British attack on the Italian fleet in November 1940, although they did away with the small formality of declaring war first. Japan's early carriers, *Akagi* and *Kaga*, were conversions of battleships but dedicated designs followed, and the *Shokaku* and *Zuikako*, completed in 1941, were probably the best of them. Thereafter, compared to the American output, production was relatively limited, and as the war progressed the crippling lack of trained aircrews meant that those carriers which were available were given only token air groups.

Each of the other major combatant nations produced carriers but most of them did not actually see any operational service. In 1927 France completed the 22,000-ton carrier *Béarn* which was converted from a Normandie class battleship hull originally laid down in 1914. Although capable of operating up to 40 aircraft, her speed of only 21 kt made her too slow for fleet work and she saw very limited service before being utilised as an aircraft transport from 1943 onwards. Two more carriers, *Joffre* and *Painlevé*, were laid down in 1938–9 but these were scrapped on the slipways after the fall of France in 1940. Germany laid down a single 28,000-ton carrier named *Graf Zeppelin* in 1936, and by 1943 she was around 90% complete. However, due to Hitler's loss of confidence in capital ships, work was abandoned and she was scuttled before the end of the war. Interestingly, her air group would have consisted of navalised Bf 109 fighters and Ju 87 dive bombers flown by Luftwaffe aircrews. There were also plans to convert two Hipper class cruisers under construction to aircraft carriers, and although some work was carried out, they never approached completion (for details, see Hipper class in the cruiser section). Italy also produced a single carrier, the *Aquila*, which was based on a converted liner. Intended to operate up to 36 aircraft, this 23,500-ton vessel was virtually complete in 1943 when Italy surrendered. She was subsequently scuttled, raised after the war and finally scrapped in 1951.

HMS Furious *in 1942. Note the raised bridge at the fore end of the flight deck. This was retracted for flying operations.* (Sydney Goodman Collection)

These three ships were originally built during World War I as shallow draught battlecruisers for use in a grandiose scheme to attack Germany's northern flank via the Baltic Sea. While *Courageous* and *Glorious* carried two twin 15in (381mm) gun mountings, *Furious* was to be armed with two single 18in (457mm) guns. However, before completion she was altered by the fitting of a flying-off deck over the bows and the forward gun turret was deleted. Trials in 1917 quickly revealed that a landing deck was also necessary and the ship was duly modified later that year. Subsequent experience with this and other ships indicated the desirability of a full-length flight deck together with hangar facilities to stow significant numbers of aircraft. Consequently, *Furious* was finally converted to a true aircraft carrier in 1921–5 and by 1939 was armed with six twin 4in (102mm) AA and three multiple 2pdr mountings. Aircraft capacity was around 30 aircraft. She had a distinguished war career but by 1944 had been eclipsed by the more modern carriers and was placed in reserve before being scrapped in 1948.

By contrast, *Courageous* and *Glorious* were completed as designed but were converted in the 1920s to aircraft carriers. Their conversion benefited from experience with *Furious* and other ships and they could operate up to 48 aircraft. Capable of high speed, they formed the core of the Royal Navy's carrier force in the 1930s but their war careers were distressingly short. *Courageous* was sunk on 17 September 1939 by torpedoes from *U-29* while carrying out an ill-advised anti-submarine sweep in the South West Approaches. *Glorious* initially fared better and contributed materially to Allied efforts in Norway in April and May 1940. When it was decided to evacuate Norway, many aircraft, including RAF high-performance Hurricane fighters, were successfully flown on board for return to the UK. Unfortunately she was intercepted by German surface forces and sunk by gunfire on 8 June. However, the successful Hurricane operations paved the way for similar aircraft to be brought into service on other carriers at a time when British naval aircraft were generally inferior to foreign contemporaries.

The battlecruiser origins of the hull are evident in this dramatic shot of HMS Courageous. *Note the anti-torpedo bulge.* (Author's Collection)

SPECIFICATION

Class: Courageous (aircraft carrier) Data *Courageous* 1939
Displacement: 22,500 tons (26,500 tons full load)
Length: 735ft (224m) pp, 786ft (239.6m); flight deck 591ft (180.1m)
Beam: 90.5ft (27.6m) over bulges, 100ft (30.5m) flight deck
Draught: 27.5ft (8.4m) full load
Machinery: 18 boilers, Parsons SR geared turbines, 4 shafts, 90,000shp
Speed: 29.5kt
Range: 5,800nm (10,740km) at 16kt
Complement: 1,360 (peacetime)
Protection: Main belt 3in (76mm), bulkheads 3in (76mm), decks 1–1.75in (25–44mm), 3in (76mm) over steering. External bulges.
Armament: 16 4.7in/119mm AA (16 × 1), 24 2pdr AA (3 × 4)
Aircraft: 48. Two catapults.
Ships in Class: Courageous (1916), Glorious (1916), Furious (1916)

HMS Hermes in 1934. Note the raised rear section of the flight deck and the large fighting top at the masthead. (Sydney Goodman Collection)

HMS Hermes, the world's first purpose-designed aircraft carrier, in 1930. (Wright & Logan Collection)

HMS *Hermes* was ordered in 1917 and has the distinction of being the first ship in the world designed from the outset as an aircraft carrier. As a matter of historical fact it was the Japanese light carrier *Hosho*, laid down after *Hermes* and completed with British assistance, which lays claim to being the first to actually enter service (although even then some evidence points to her being originally laid down as an oil tanker). *Hermes* commissioned in 1923 and she was the first carrier to introduce the concept of an island superstructure, complete with funnel, on the starboard side. This left an uninterrupted flight deck and ensured that gases from the funnel were kept well clear of flying operations. Although successful in concept, she was far too small for major operations and her aircraft complement was constrained by limited hangar capacity and restricted lift dimensions. By the outbreak of World War II she carried only 12 Swordfish aircraft and no fighters, and was employed mainly in the South Atlantic and Indian oceans hunting Axis raiders. She was sunk off Ceylon (Sri Lanka) on 9 April 1942 by Japanese aircraft from Admiral Nagumo's Carrier Striking Force, which had made a successful foray into the Indian Ocean at that time.

SPECIFICATION

Class: Hermes (aircraft carrier) Data 1941
Displacement: 10,850 tons (13,000 tons full load)
Length: 548ft (167m) pp, 600ft (182.9m) oa
Beam: 70.25ft (21.4m) over bulges
Draught: 21.5ft (6.5m) full load
Machinery: 6 Yarrow boilers, 2 shafts, Parsons SR geared turbines, 40,000shp
Speed: 25kt
Range: n/a
Complement: 664
Protection: Main belt 1.5–2in (38–51mm), decks 1in (25mm). External bulges.
Armament: 6 5.5in/140mm (6 × 1), 4 4in/102mm AA (4 × 1), 4 2pdr AA (1 × 4).
Aircraft: 12
Ships in Class: *Hermes* (1919)

35

With two funnels, HMS Eagle *had an unusual profile for an aircraft carrier. The after 6in (152mm) guns are visible at the stern below the flight deck.* (Sydney Goodman Collection)

By the end of World War I the British Admiralty was thoroughly convinced of the value of aircraft carriers and actively sought to expand its fleet. In 1917 the incomplete Chilean battleship *Almirante Cochrane*, whose construction on the River Tyne had been suspended in 1914, was purchased with the intention of converting her to an aircraft carrier. She eventually commissioned in 1925 and adopted the island superstructure layout although, uniquely, this was surmounted by two funnels. The original battleship hull was heavily armoured and 6in (152mm) guns were fitted which together gave the ship some chance of defending herself against surface attack, although if properly employed no carrier should find herself in such a situation. The battleship hull was not easily altered to incorporate a good-sized hangar and consequently aircraft capacity was only 24, and this was reduced to around 21 by 1942 when she was employed as part of Force H in the Mediterranean engaged in convoy operations in support of Malta. In August of that year, Operation Pedestal was mounted with no fewer than four British carriers taking part. It was during this operation that *Eagle* was hit by four torpedoes from the German *U-73* and sank in fewer than eight minutes.

Although it was not realised at the time, she was the last British fleet carrier to be lost during World War II.

SPECIFICATION:

Class: Eagle (aircraft carrier) Data 1942
Displacement: 22,600 tons (26,880 tons full load)
Length: 627ft (191.1m) pp, 667.5ft (203.5m); flight deck 652 × 96ft (198.7 × 29.3m)
Beam: 93ft (28.3m); 105.25ft (32.1m) over bulges
Draught: 25.5ft (7.8m) full load
Machinery: 32 boilers, 4 shafts, HP and LP turbines, 50,000shp
Speed: 24kt
Range: 4,000nm (7,400 km) at 18kt
Complement: 745 (ship)
Protection: Main belt 4–7in (102–178mm), bulkheads 4in (102mm), decks 0.5–2in (13–51mm), gunshields 1in (25mm). External bulges.
Armament: 9 6in/152mm (9 × 1), 4 4in/102mm AA (4 × 1), 16 2pdr AA (2 × 8), 16 20mm/0.8in AA.
Aircraft: 24
Ships in Class: Eagle (1918)

Ark Royal

Completed in 1938, HMS Ark Royal was one of the most advanced aircraft carriers of her time. (Sydney Goodman Collection)

Laid down in 1935, the *Ark Royal* was one of the best pre-war carrier designs of any nation and drew heavily from the wealth of experience gained in operating the various preceding ships. The displacement was set at 22,000 tons, although at the time the design was drawn up the treaty limit on aircraft carriers was set at 27,000 tons, reduced by the second London Naval Treaty (1935) to 23,000 tons. As completed, *Ark Royal* was a handsome ship although her lines were slightly spoilt by a significant overhang of the after end of the flight deck. Rightly appreciating that the major threat to carriers was from air attack, the AA armament of 16 4.5in (114mm) guns plus numerous light AA was excellent for that period and well in advance of foreign contemporaries. Thanks to a two-deck hangar layout, aircraft capacity was set at 72, again well up to international standards but the supply of suitable British aircraft was always problematic and she rarely ever carried more than 50.

As Britain's premier carrier, she had a very active war including operations off Norway, and she was later instrumental in the successful chase to sink the *Bismarck*, her aircraft scoring the torpedo hits which slowed down the German battleship so that she could be engaged by units of the Home Fleet. Later she was engaged in operations in the Mediterranean where she was hit by a single torpedo from the German *U-81* on 13 November 1941 when only 30 miles from Gibraltar. Despite

attempts to save her, it proved impossible to prevent water flooding into the boiler uptakes and she subsequently sank the following day while under tow. At least the Royal Navy learnt some valuable lessons in respect of damage control aboard aircraft carriers, and these were put to good use later in the war.

SPECIFICATION

Class: Ark Royal (aircraft carrier) Data as built
Displacement: 22,000 tons (27,720 tons full load)
Length: 685ft (208.8m) pp, 800ft (243.8m) oa; flight deck 797 × 96ft (242.9 × 29.3m)
Beam: 95ft (29m)
Draught: 28ft (8.5m) full load
Machinery: 6 boilers, 3 shafts, Parsons SR turbines, 102,000shp
Speed: 30.5kt
Range: 7,600mm (14,075 km) at 20kt
Complement: 1,636 (inc. air group)
Protection: Main belt 4.5in (114mm), bulkheads 2.5in (64mm), decks 2.5–3.5in (64–89mm)
Armament: 16 4.5in/114mm DP (8 × 2), 48 2pdr AA (6 × 8), 32 0.5in/13mm AA (8 × 4)
Aircraft: 72 maximum, normally not more than 50 embarked. Two catapults.
Ships in Class: Ark Royal (1937)

*HMS **Formidable** was completed in November 1941 and played a major part in the Battle of Matapan, March 1941. (Author's Collection)*

Although similar in size to the preceding *Ark Royal*, this group of carriers differed in that the flight deck, hangar sides and bulkheads were heavily armoured to the extent that they should be able to withstand direct hits by 1,000lb (450kg) bombs. This feature undoubtedly saved most of them at one time or another. *Illustrious* was hit by no fewer than eight bombs in an attack by German dive bombers in June 1941 and survived, although repairs took almost 12 months. In the closing stages of the war all six were allocated to the British Pacific Fleet, and although hit many times by kamikaze attacks were rarely out of action for more than a few hours, in contrast to the US carriers where such damage was usually a pass-

port to a few months in Pearl Harbor Naval Yard. The protection afforded by the armoured deck was not without penalty, and the first three vessels had only a single hangar deck so that aircraft capacity was reduced to 36 (compared to *Ark Royal's* 72). This was rectified to some extent with the fourth ship, *Indomitable*, which incorporated a lower half-length hangar increasing the aircraft complement to 48. Revised aircraft handling arrangements during World War II eventually meant that all four could operate up to 54 aircraft. The last pair, *Indefatigable* and *Implacable*, reverted to two full-length hangars and their eventual aircraft complement was 81, although they did not commission until 1944.

*HMS **Indomitable** in 1943 with Seafire and Albacore torpedo bombers ranged on deck. (Sydney Goodman Collection)*

SPECIFICATION

Class: Illustrious (aircraft carrier) Data *Illustrious* as built
Displacement: 23,200 tons (28,620 tons full load)
Length: 673ft (205.1m) pp, 744ft (226.8m) oa; flight deck 747 × 95ft (227.7 × 29m)
Beam: 96ft (29.3m)
Draught: 28ft (8.5m) full load
Machinery: 6 boilers, 3 shafts, Parsons SR turbines, 111,000shp
Speed: 30.5kt
Range: 11,000nm (20,370km) at 14kt
Complement: 1,500
Protection: Main belt 4.5in (114mm), bulkheads 2.5in (64mm), lower deck 3in (76mm). Flight deck 3in (76mm), hangar sides 4.5in (114mm), hangar bulkheads 2.5–4.5in (64–114mm)
Armament: 16 4.5in/114mm DP (8 × 2), 48 2pdr AA (6 × 8), 8 20mm/0.8in AA
Aircraft: 36, later increased to 54.
Ships in Class: Illustrious (1939), Victorious (1939), Formidable (1939), Indomitable (1940), Implacable (1942), Indefatigable (1942)

A pre-war view of the USS Saratoga *showing the original 8in (203mm) guns fore and aft of the island. The black stripe on the funnel distinguished her from her sister ship,* Lexington. *(Eric Buehler Naval Aviation Library)*

These two vessels were originally laid down in 1920–1 as part of a class of six 43,500-ton battlecruisers and would have been armed with eight 16in (406mm) and 16 6in (152mm) guns. However, under the terms of the 1921 Washington Naval Treaty four were scrapped while still on the slipway and work on the two most advanced hulls was suspended as plans were drawn up to convert them to aircraft carriers. Subsequently the *Lexington* and *Saratoga* were launched in 1925 and were commissioned in 1927. The original armament included eight 8in (203mm) guns in twin turrets fore and aft of the island superstructure and the single massive funnel. The huge size of the battlecruiser hull allowed the construction of a spacious hangar covered by a full-length flight deck, and consequently these ships proved capable of stowing and operating large numbers of aircraft including the larger and heavier types developed during World War II.

During the late 1920s and 1930s, the two ships formed the backbone of US naval aviation and proved the tactical doctrines which helped to make the US Navy the foremost protagonists of naval airpower. Both ships were fully employed in the aftermath of Pearl Harbor, but the *Lexington* was lost during the Battle of the Coral Sea in May 1942 as a result of attacks by Japanese carrier-based aircraft. The *Saratoga* was more fortunate and survived being hit by a submarine torpedo in January 1942. During the subsequent refit the 8in guns were removed and the light AA armament boosted. She was active throughout the war despite again being torpedoed off Guadalcanal in August 1942, and being severely damaged by four kamikaze suicide bombers in February 1945, losing 123 crew members. Having survived all that the Japanese could throw at her, she was eventually discarded as a target in the 1946 atomic bomb tests at Bikini Atoll.

A late wartime view of Saratoga. *The original armament has been removed and replaced by four twin 5in (127mm) AA.* (Eric Buehler Naval Aviation Library)

SPECIFICATION

Class: Lexington (aircraft carrier) Data *Saratoga* 1942
Displacement: 33,000 tons (39,000 tons full load)
Length: 830ft (253m) wl, 888ft (270.7m) oa; flight deck 901ft (274.6m)
Beam: 105.5ft (32.2m) (hull), 130ft (39.6m) (flight deck)
Draught: 32ft (9.8m) full load
Machinery: 16 boilers, General Electric turbo generators, 8 electric motors, 4 shafts, 184,000shp.
Speed: 33kt
Range: 8,015nm (14,840km) at 20kt
Complement: 3,300
Protection: Main belt 6in (152mm), bulkheads 6in (152mm), main deck 3in (76mm). Turrets 3in (76mm). Barbettes 6in (152mm).
Armament: 8 5in/127mm DP (4 x 2), 96 40mm/1.6in AA (24 x 4), 32 20mm/0.8in (32 x 1)
Aircraft: 90
Ships in Class: *Lexington* (1925), *Saratoga* (1925)

USS Ranger (CV 4) as completed. Note the raised funnels at the after end of the flight deck. (Eric Buehler Naval Aviation Library)

The *Ranger* was laid down in September 1931 and was the first purpose-designed US Navy aircraft carrier. At a standard displacement of 14,500 tons she was substantially below the upper treaty limit of 22,000 tons for this type of vessel. However, she clearly demonstrated that the US Navy had already espoused the basic premise that a carrier's prime role was to operate aircraft, and she could stow up to a maximum of 86. This was achieved at the expense of armour protection and a relatively slow speed. Although a standard island superstructure on the starboard side was adopted, the machinery was placed aft and the boiler uptakes vented through hinged funnels on either side of the flight deck. This was a common feature of early carriers but was less than satisfactory in service.

Due to her relatively small size, *Ranger* was not a good seaboat and was severely limited in her ability to operate aircraft in rough weather. Consequently she saw relatively little frontline operational service after America entered the war in 1941 and was used variously as a training carrier or as an aircraft transport, although in 1943 she operated with the British Home Fleet in strikes against German shipping off Norway. She survived the war and was scrapped in 1947.

SPECIFICATION

Class: Ranger (aircraft carrier) Data as completed 1934
Displacement: 14,500 tons
Length: 728ft (221.9m) wl, 769ft (234.4) oa
Beam: 80ft (24.4m); flight deck 109.5ft (33.4m)
Draught: 20ft (6.1m) (standard)
Machinery: 6 boilers, Curtiss HP and Parsons LP geared turbines, 2 shafts, 53,500shp
Speed: 29.5kt
Range: 11,500nm (21,300km) at 15kt
Complement: 2,000
Protection: Main belt 2in (51mm), bulkheads 2in (51mm), main deck 1in (25mm)
Armament: 8 5in/127mm AA (8 × 1)
Aircraft: 86
Ships in Class: *Ranger* (1933)

Yorktown

Even while *Ranger* was under construction it was decided that larger and better protected vessels were required and the result was the two ships of the Yorktown class laid down in 1934. A more conventional machinery arrangement was adopted with the single broad funnel incorporated into the island superstructure. A third ship, *Hornet*, was laid down in 1939 to a slightly modified design with a larger flight deck. These ships were over 4kt faster than the *Ranger* and were better able to operate aircraft under rough conditions.

With the disabling of most of the US battlefleet at Pearl Harbor in 1941, these three carriers became a vital part of the American naval effort in the Pacific and were heavily engaged. *Yorktown* played a vital role in the Battle of the Coral Sea in May 1942, although she was damaged. A Herculean effort by the Pearl Harbor Naval Yard got her back into action for the vital Battle of Midway where her aircraft sank the Japanese carrier *Soryu* before the *Yorktown* herself was damaged by air attack and later finished off with a submarine torpedo. *Hornet* delivered the famous Doolittle raid on Tokyo in April 1942 and was also present at Midway before being eventually sunk by multiple torpedo hits off Santa Cruz on 27 October 1942. On the other hand, *Enterprise* had a charmed life and was present at Midway, Guadalcanal and Santa Cruz. In May 1945 she was hit by a kamikaze and, although repaired, saw no further wartime service. She was eventually scrapped in 1958, perhaps the most famous of all the US World War II carriers.

Wasp

The Washington Naval Treaty limited the US Navy to 135,000 tons for aircraft carriers. Allowing for the *Lexington*, *Saratoga*, *Ranger* and two Yorktown vessels, the remaining tonnage was approximately 15,000 which immediately set the limit for the next to be built, USS *Wasp*. Laid down in April 1936, she was completed almost exactly four years later. Although incorporating many features of the preceding Yorktown class, in overall size she was similar to the *Ranger* and suffered from the same disadvantages. Consequently she was initially deployed to the Atlantic and in 1942 joined the British Royal Navy in operations to fly Spitfire fighter aircraft to the besieged Mediterranean island of Malta. However, the serious carrier losses in the Pacific led to her being redeployed to support operations around Guadalcanal in the south-west Pacific. Here she was hit by three torpedoes from the Japanese submarine *I-19* and the resulting fires caused her to be abandoned. Subsequently she was finished off and sunk by torpedoes from the US destroyer *Lansdowne*.

USS Wasp *(CV 7) was commissioned in 1940. (Eric Buehler Naval Aviation Library)*

The Yorktown *(CV 5) alongside with a full complement of aircraft parked on the flight deck. (Eric Buehler Naval Aviation Library)*

SPECIFICATION

Class: Yorktown (aircraft carrier) Data *Yorktown* 1942
Displacement: 19,800 tons (25,000 tons full load)
Length: 761ft (232m) wl, 809.5ft (246.7m) oa
Beam: 83ft (25.3m); flight deck 109ft (33.2m)
Draught: 28ft (8.5m) full load
Machinery: 9 boilers, Parsons geared turbines, 4 shafts, 120,000shp
Speed: 33kt
Range: 8,220nm (15,220km) at 20kt
Complement: 2,919
Protection: Main belt 4in (102mm), bulkheads 4in (102mm), main deck 3in (76mm)
Armament: 8 5in/127mm AA (8 × 1), 16 1.1in/28mm AA (4 × 4), 16 0.5in/13mm AA (4 × 4)
Aircraft: 81 to 90
Ships in Class: *Yorktown* (1936), *Enterprise* (1936), *Hornet* (1940)

SPECIFICATION

Class: Wasp (aircraft carrier) Data 1942
Displacement: 14,700 tons (21,000 tons full load)
Length: 688ft (209.7m) wl, 741ft (225.9m) oa
Beam: 80.75ft (24.6m); flight deck 109ft (33.2m)
Draught: 28ft (8.5m) full load
Machinery: 6 boilers, Parsons geared turbines, 2 shafts, 75,000shp
Speed: 29.5kt
Range: 8,000nm (14,820km) at 20kt
Complement: 2,367
Protection: Main belt 4in (102mm), bulkheads 4in (102mm), main and lower decks 1.5in (38mm)
Armament: 8 5in/127mm AA (8 × 1), 16 1.1in/28mm AA (4 × 4), 30 20mm/0.8in AA (30 × 1), 9 0.5in/13mm AA.
Aircraft: 84
Ships in Class: *Wasp* (1939)

USS Essex (CV 9), lead ship of the class, with a strike force of Corsairs and Helldivers ranged on deck. (Eric Buehler Naval Aviation Library)

The Essex class carriers eventually provided the US Navy with the striking forces it needed to sweep across the Pacific to victory in 1945. The name ship was originally envisaged as a slightly enlarged *Hornet*, but the lapsing of treaty limitations, together with requirements to operate larger aircraft (which needed more support, fuel and armaments), led to an increase of almost one-third in displacement. The result was a thoroughly seaworthy vessel which was well protected and carried a strong defensive armament, while still able to operate over 90 aircraft. Operations were assisted by the provision of two centreline lifts and one portside deck edge lift. Vessels completed during the war were built in two groups, the second featuring a lengthened bow to give better arcs of fire to the forward 40mm (1.6in) guns.

Despite being involved in many major actions, none of the Essex class was lost during the war although some were severely damaged by both conventional and kamikaze attacks. The most dramatic example was the USS *Franklin* which was hit by two 500lb (225kg) bombs on 19 March 1945. These penetrated to the hangar deck and caused aircraft, bombs and fuel to explode, wreaking fearful damage and starting massive fires. Casualties included 832 dead and 270 wounded. Eventually the fires were brought under control and the ship was taken to Pearl Harbor for repairs. In the post-war era, the class showed the soundness of the basic design and many were successfully adapted to operate jet aircraft, remaining in service until the early 1970s.

SPECIFICATION

Class: Essex (aircraft carrier) Data *Essex* as completed 1942
Displacement: 27,100 tons (33,000 tons full load)
Length: 840ft (256m) wl, 876ft (267m) oa
Beam: 93ft (28.3m); flight deck 147.5ft (45m)
Draught: 28.5ft (8.7m)
Machinery: 8 boilers, Westinghouse turbines, 150,000shp
Speed: 33kt
Range: 14,100nm (26,110km) at 20kt
Complement: 3,448
Protection: Main belt 2–3in (51–76m), bulkheads 2–3in (51–76m), flight deck 1.5in (38mm), hangar deck 3in (76mm), main deck 1.5in (38mm). Turrets and barbettes 1.5in (38mm).
Armament: 12 5in/127mm AA (4 × 2, 4 × 1), 68 40mm/1.6in AA (17 × 4), 52 20mm/0.8in AA (52 × 1).
Aircraft: 80 to 100
Ships in Class: 1st Group: *Essex, Lexington, Bunker Hill* (1942), *Yorktown, Intrepid, Hornet, Franklin, Wasp* (1943); *Bennington, Bon Homme Richard* (1944). 2nd Group: *Ticonderoga, Randolph, Hancock, Boxer, Antietam, Shangri-La, Lake Champlain* (1944); *Leyte, Kearsage, Princeton, Tarawa, Valley Forge, Philippine Sea* (1945). 3rd Group: *Oriskany* (1945).

An Essex class carrier showing the disruptive Measure 32 camouflage scheme applied to many of these ships.
(Eric Buehler Naval Aviation Library)

The Independence class aircraft carriers were rapidly produced using hulls originally laid down as Cleveland class cruisers. Photo shows USS Independence *in 1944. (Eric Buehler Naval Aviation Library)*

By 1941 it was apparent that the US Navy would be engaged in a major Pacific war within a relatively short period and a shortage of aircraft carriers would be inevitable until sufficient of the new Essex class could be built. As an interim measure it was decided to produce a small carrier based on the hull and machinery of the 10,000-ton Cleveland class cruiser (cf). The resulting carriers were something of a compromise with limited hangar capacity and a short flight deck. A small island superstructure was installed well forward on the starboard side and the boilers vented through four smokestacks angled outboard, again on the starboard side. Although intended to operate up to 45 aircraft, in practice this was reduced to around 30 for operational purposes, although when acting in the aircraft transport role around 100 could be stowed.

All nine vessels were completed in 1943 and they played a valuable role in the build-up of forces for the great offensives of 1944 and 1945. The USS *Princeton* was the only war casualty, sunk by Japanese air attack off Leyte on 24 October 1944. Many of the others were also damaged at various times but survived the war, and two were subsequently loaned to France (*Belleau Wood* and *Langley*) and another to Spain (*Cabot*).

SPECIFICATION

Class: Independence (aircraft carrier) Data *Independence* as completed 1943
Displacement: 11,000 tons (15,100 tons full load)
Length: 600ft (182.9m) wl, 622.5ft (189.7m) oa
Beam: 71.5ft (21.8m); flight deck 109.25ft (33.3m)
Draught: 26ft (7.9m) full load
Machinery: 4 boilers, General Electric geared turbines, 4 shafts, 100,000shp
Speed: 32kt
Range: 7,600nm (14,075km) at 20kt
Complement: 1,560
Protection: Main belt 5in (127mm) (max), bulkheads 5in (127mm), main deck 3in (76mm), lower deck 2in (51mm).
Armament: Four 5in/127mm AA (4 × 1), 26 40mm/1.6in AA (2 × 4, 9 × 2), 40 20mm/0.8in AA (40 × 1)
Aircraft: 45
Ships in Class: *Independence, Princeton, Belleau Wood* (1942); *Cowpens, Monterey, Langley, Cabot, Bataan, San Jacinto* (1943)

UNITED STATES/UNITED KINGDOM
Bogue/Prince William

USS Bogue (CVE 9), the name ship of a class of 21 escort carriers built for the British and US navies. (Eric Buehler Naval Aviation Library)

The concept of a small aircraft carrier able to accompany and protect ocean convoys originated with the Royal Navy in 1940. Subsequently the US Navy converted six modern merchant ships as escort carriers (Long Island class) of which four were immediately transferred to the British. Thereafter production centred on purpose-built vessels which closely followed the lines of the mercantile conversions. The first of these (Bogue class, described below) were powered by steam turbines and 11 of the 21 built were transferred to the Royal Navy. The following Prince William class featured an improved AA armament but were otherwise repeats, and all but one were also transferred to

the RN. Entering service during 1943, they helped to swing the balance in the Battle of the Atlantic in the Allies' favour. While almost all of the foregoing were built for the RN, the US Navy commissioned no fewer than 50 Casablanca class CVEs (escort carrier) in the space of 12 months from mid-1943 – a staggering rate of production. These ships were very similar to their RN counterparts except that reciprocating machinery replaced the steam turbines. The final CVE design was the Commencement Bay class, produced from 1944 onwards, which featured a longer hull and flight deck, displacement rising to 11,300 tons, and were capable of operating 34 aircraft.

The USS Gambier Bay (CVE 73), a Casablanca class escort carrier, was sunk by Japanese cruisers on 25 October 1944 during the Battle of Samar. (Eric Buehler Naval Aviation Library)

SPECIFICATION

Class: Bogue/Prince William (escort carrier) Data Bogue class
Displacement: 7,800 tons (15,400 tons full load)
Length: 465ft (141.7m) wl, 495.75ft (151.1m) oa
Beam: 69.5ft (21.2m); flight deck 111ft (33.8m)
Draught: 26ft (7.9m) full load
Machinery: 2 boilers, Allis Chalmers geared turbines, 1 shaft, 8,500shp
Speed: 18kt
Range: 26,000nm (48,150km) at 15kt
Complement: 890
Protection: nil
Armament: Two 5in/127mm AA (2 × 1), 8 40mm/1.6in AA (4 × 2), 12 20mm/0.8in AA (12 × 1)
Aircraft: 28
Ships in Class: Bogue class: 21 ships (1941–2); Prince William class: 24 ships (1942–3)

The carrier Akagi was produced by converting a battlecruiser hull. Unusually, her island superstructure was on the port side of the flight deck. (US Navy Historical Branch)

The Japanese were quick to realise the potential of the aircraft carrier and initially drew heavily on British experience during the closing stages of World War I. Like the US and British navies, they subsequently converted capital ships, redundant under the naval treaties, to fast aircraft carriers. The ships selected for conversion were the *Akagi* and *Amagi*, originally laid down in 1920 as 41,000-ton battlecruisers armed with 16in (406mm) guns. The *Amagi* was damaged beyond repair by an earthquake while still on the slipway, but *Akagi* eventually entered service in 1927. Initially she had two flying-off decks below the main flight deck but these were removed during a major refit 1935–8. To Western eyes she was unusual in that the small island superstructure was offset to port while the boiler gases were discharged through a huge funnel curved downwards on the starboard side.

Akagi was the flagship of the Japanese carrier force which carried out the Pearl Harbor attack, but she was later sunk by American aircraft at Midway in June 1942. The destruction of the *Amagi* in 1923 led to the selection of the *Kaga*, an ex-40,000-ton

battleship, as a replacement. As originally completed in 1928, she also featured multiple flying-off decks but she was subsequently refitted in the 1930s with a single flight deck and a small island on the starboard side. She was considerably slower than the *Akagi*, which made combined tactical operations difficult. Displacing some 30,000 tons, she was armed with 16 5in (127mm) AA guns and could carry up to 72 aircraft, although this reduced to around 60 by 1941 when she formed part of the Pearl Harbor striking force. Like her half sister, *Kaga* was lost at the Battle of Midway in June 1942.

A view of Kaga clearly showing the downward-angled funnel on the starboard side.

A model of the Kaga showing the flight deck layout. The red and white stripes on the round-down were a common feature of Japanese carriers.

SPECIFICATION

Class: Kaga/Akagi (aircraft carrier) Data *Akagi* 1941
Displacement: 36,500 tons (41,300 tons full load)
Length: 771ft (235m) pp, 855.5ft (260.8m) oa; flight deck 818ft (249.3m)
Beam: 102.75ft (31.3m) over bulges; flight deck 100ft (30.5m)
Draught: 28ft (8.5m) (mean)
Machinery: 19 boilers, Gijutsu-Hombu turbines, 4 shafts, 133,000shp
Speed: 31.5kt
Range: 8,000nm (14,820km) at 14kt
Complement: 2,000
Protection: Main belt 6in (152mm), main deck 3in (76mm). External bulges.
Armament: 6 8in/203mm (6 × 1), 12 4.7in/119mm AA (6 × 2), 28 25mm/1in AA (14 × 2)
Aircraft: 91 (maximum)
Ships in Class: *Kaga* (1921), *Akagi* (1925)

The Shoho *was originally completed as a submarine depot ship but was converted into an aircraft carrier in 1941–2.*
(WZ Bilddienst)

In the 1930s Japan began a major build-up of her carrier forces but, partly because of treaty limitations and partly because of their obsession with secrecy, a number of ships were laid down as seaplane carriers, depot ships and oil tankers, each with the potential to be converted to an aircraft carrier at future date. The first of this type were the two Shoho class laid down in 1934–5 as 9,500-ton submarine depot ships, followed by two larger (11,000 tons) Chitose class seaplane tenders (1934–6). *Shoho*, originally named *Tsurugisaki*, was actually completed to the original design in 1939 but was rebuilt as a carrier in 1941–2. *Zuiho* (ex-*Takasaki*) was modified while building and did not commission until 1941. As carriers they had a full-length flight deck with the funnel venting downwards on the starboard side. There was no island, the ship being conned from a bridge deck below the forward end of the flight deck.

In service, the *Shoho* was sunk by aircraft from the USS *Yorktown* in the Battle of the Coral Sea (7 May 1942), thus gaining the dubious distinction of being the first Japanese carrier loss of the war. *Zuiho* had a more active war but was badly damaged at Santa Cruz on 25 October 1942. She was soon repaired and was involved in actions off Guadalcanal and the Marianas before being sunk by a combination of bombs and torpedoes off Cape Engano in the battles around Leyte Gulf in October 1944. In contrast, both *Chitose* and *Chiyoda* saw service as seaplane carriers before being converted to aircraft carriers in 1942–4. Their basic configuration was similar to the Shoho class but their smaller size meant they could carry only 24 aircraft. Their career as aircraft carriers was short-lived and both were sunk off Cape Engano at the same time as the *Zuiho*.

SPECIFICATION

Class: Shoho/Chitose (aircraft carrier) Data *Zuiho* 1944
Displacement: 11,262 tons (14,200 tons full load)
Length: 661ft (201.5m) wl, 674.25ft (205.5m) oa; flight deck 632ft (192.6m)
Beam: 60ft (18.3m) (hull), 75.5ft (23m) (flight deck)
Draught: 21.75ft (6.6m) (mean)
Machinery: 4 boilers, Kanpon geared turbines, 2 shafts, 52,000shp
Speed: 28kt
Range: 7,800nm (14,450km) at 18kt
Complement: 785
Armament: 8 5in/127mm AA (4 × 2), 68 25mm/1in AA, 6 8-barrelled AA rocket launchers.
Aircraft: 30
Ships in Class: *Shoho* (1935), *Zuiho* (1936), *Chitose* (1936), *Chiyoda* (1937)

The carrier Zuikaku *as completed in 1941.* (US Navy Historical Branch)

Shokaku *(shown here) and her sister ship* Zuikaku *were among the most successful of the Japanese carriers.* (US Navy Historical Branch)

These two carriers, completed in 1941, were perhaps the best of the Japanese carriers and built on experience gained with the Soryu class. With a standard displacement of over 25,000 tons, they were considerably larger than the earlier vessels and could therefore operate more aircraft. The hull was heavily armoured but the flight deck was virtually unprotected and experience was to show that the arrangements for stowage of aviation fuel, always a problem aboard aircraft carriers, were flawed. During the war both ships had the light AA armament supplemented by the addition of single and triple 25mm (1in) AA mountings, and both received a radar outfit in 1943–4 (at a time when a complex radar outfit was standard aboard all major Allied warships). In July 1944 *Zuikaku*'s AA protection included no fewer than 96 25mm guns and 168 5in (127mm) rocket launchers in six multiple mountings carried in the bows.

Both carriers were part of the Pearl Harbor striking force and, indeed, it was more than likely that the operation was timed to coincide with their joining the fleet. *Shokaku*'s aircraft were responsible for sinking the USS *Lexington* at the Battle of the Coral Sea but she was seriously damaged herself and was barely able to make it back to Japan for repairs. At Santa Cruz (October 1942), she was hit again by six bombs but survived. Fate finally caught up with her at the Battle of the Philippine Sea where she was sunk on 19 June 1944 by four torpedoes from a US submarine. *Zuikaku* was also present at the Coral Sea but was not damaged. In the Battle

of the Philippine Sea she was seriously damaged by air attack and it was only heroic efforts from the crew which eventually contained the petrol fires which threatened to engulf the ship. By October 1944, the once proud ship was effectively reduced to acting as a decoy and was sunk by sustained air attack off Cape Engano during the Leyte Gulf operations.

SPECIFICATION:

Class: Shokaku (aircraft carrier) Data *Shokaku* as completed 1941
Displacement: 25,675 tons (32,100 tons full load)
Length: 820.25ft (250m) wl, 845ft (257.6m) oa; flight deck 787ft (239.9m)
Beam: 85.5ft (26.1m) (hull), 95ft (29m) (flight deck)
Draught: 29ft (8.8m) (mean)
Machinery: 8 boilers, Kanpon geared turbines, 4 shafts, 160,000shp
Speed: 34kt
Range: 10,000nm (18,520km) at 18kt
Complement: 1,660
Protection: Main belt 6.5in (16.5m), decks 5in (127mm) over magazines and 4in (102mm) over machinery
Armament: 16 5in/127mm AA (8 × 2), 36 25mm/1in AA (12 × 3)
Aircraft: 84
Ships in Class: *Shokaku, Zuikaku* (1939)

The carrier Hiryu *running trials in 1939. (US Navy Historical Branch)*

Although similar in size and aircraft capacity, these two ships were not identical sisters. The design could be traced back to a 1932 project for a heavily armed cruiser with a flight deck which, for treaty purposes, would not count as an aircraft carrier. However, Japan subsequently decided to ignore any treaty limitations and set about building two 16,000-ton carriers of which the first, *Soryu*, was laid down in 1934 and completed in 1937, while the other, *Hiryu*, followed two years later. *Soryu* featured two hangar decks and had a small island superstructure conventionally sited on the starboard side while the two funnels were angled downwards, again on the starboard side. The flight deck was served by three lifts and 63 operational aircraft could be carried, with another nine stored in reserve. Subsequently construction of the *Hiryu* benefited from experience with *Soryu* and other ships and she had a strengthened hull with increased armour protection so that standard displacement rose to around 17,500 tons. A noticeable difference was the locating of an enlarged island superstructure on the port side, although the funnels remained to starboard. There were also some differences in the disposition of the 5in (127mm) guns and light AA armament. Aircraft capacity was 64 plus nine in reserve.

The two ships operated together for the whole of their careers, both forming part of the Pearl Harbor striking force and then taking part in the foray into the Indian Ocean to strike at British forces around Ceylon. Subsequently they took part in the battle of Midway and were lost to attacks from American dive bombers.

SPECIFICATION

Class: Soryu (aircraft carrier) Data *Soryu* as completed 1937
Displacement: 15,900 tons (18,800 tons full load)
Length: 728ft (221.9m) wl, 746.5ft (227.5m) oa; flight deck 705.5ft (215m)
Beam: 70ft (21.3m) (hull), 85.5ft (26.1m) (flight deck)
Draught: 25ft (7.6m) (mean)
Machinery: 8 boilers, Kanpon geared turbines, 4 shafts, 152,000shp
Speed: 34.5kt
Range: 7,750nm (14,350km) at 18kt
Complement: 1,100
Protection: Main belt 1.75in (44mm), decks 1in (25mm) (2in/51mm over magazine)
Armament: 12 5in/127mm AA (6 × 2), 28 25mm/1in AA (14 × 2)
Aircraft: 72 (maximum)
Ships in Class: *Soryu* (1935), *Hiryu* (1937)

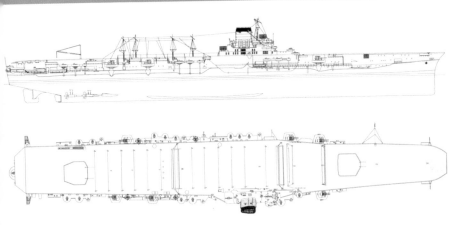

Taiho. *Deck plan and profile.*

Unlike the British and Americans, the Japanese never managed to produce a standard class of fleet carrier and continued to produce one-offs and conversions of auxiliaries and merchant ships. One of the few major purpose-built carriers to be completed during World War II was the 29,000-ton *Taiho* which, apart from the converted battleship *Shinano*, was also the largest to be completed during that period. In profile she superficially resembled the British Illustrious class and shared with them the concept of an armoured flight deck. This latter feature restricted hangar size and consequently the aircraft complement was officially only around 60, although more could be stowed in reserve. The flight deck was served by two lifts and the substantial island superstructure was mounted on the starboard side with the large funnel canted outwards.

Laid down in July 1941, *Taiho* was completed in March 1944 and became the flagship of the First Carrier Strike Force of the Combined Fleet. However, her active career was extremely short as she was torpedoed by the US submarine *Albacore* during the Battle of the Philippine Sea (June 1944). The ship survived the initial torpedo impact for several hours as the damage control parties fought to keep the ship afloat. However, a concentration of vapours from damaged aviation fuel storage tanks was eventually ignited by an

electrical spark and the resulting massive explosion tore the ship apart. Although *Taiho* was the sole example of her type, two more slightly larger versions were ordered in 1942 but were cancelled before construction began.

SPECIFICATION

Class: Taiho (aircraft carrier) Data as completed 1944
Displacement: 29,300 tons (37,250 tons full load)
Length: 830ft (253m) wl, 855ft (260.6m) oa; flight deck 843ft (256.9m)
Beam: 91ft (27.7m) (hull), 98.5ft (30m) (flight deck)
Draught: 31.5ft (9.6m) (mean)
Machinery: 8 boilers, Kanpon geared turbines, 4 shafts, 152,000shp
Speed: 33kt
Range: 8,000nm (14,820km) at 18kt
Complement: 1,751
Protection: Main belt 6in (152mm), main deck 5in (127mm) over machinery spaces, flight deck 3in (76mm)
Armament: 12 3.9in/99mm AA (6 × 2), 51 25mm/1in (17 × 3)
Aircraft: 53 (standard), 74 (maximum)
Ships in Class: Taiho (1943)

CRUISERS

Prior to World War II, the traditional roles of the cruiser were scouting, supporting the destroyer flotillas in fleet actions, and the disruption or protection of trade routes. The increasing influence of the aeroplane on naval operations resulted in a change of emphasis in these areas and this had a direct effect on the type of cruiser built before and during the war. Certainly the task of scouting and reconnaissance could be better carried out by aircraft, and consequently in the pre-war era most cruisers carried at least one aircraft while the US and Japanese navies commonly shipped at least three or four aircraft to cover the vast tracts of the Pacific. However, as the war progressed, a combination of carrier-based aircraft and radar took over this role and aircraft facilities were scaled down or removed.

Also, while aircraft played an increasingly important part in naval battles, traditional surface actions became increasingly rare. Certainly the concept of massed destroyer flotillas led by cruisers attacking an enemy fleet never occurred in the form envisaged by pre-war naval strategists. In the trade protection role, those nations such as Britain that depended heavily on seaborne trade obviously needed to protect those vital lifelines, and prior to World War II the British Admiralty declared a requirement for at least 70 cruisers to cover worldwide commitments, although it was never to reach that total as new construc-

tion barely kept pace with the early war losses.

As with other warship types, the size and armament of cruisers was heavily determined by naval treaties. While the 1922 Washington Naval Treaty set no specific limits on cruiser size, it did state that any vessel displacing more than 10,000 tons and armed with guns greater than 8 in (203mm) calibre would be classed as a capital ship and included in the overall allowances for such vessels. This effectively defined a cruiser, and all major navies set about designing and building 10,000-ton, 8in-gun cruisers. However, such ships were large and expensive, and did not necessarily meet requirements for many of the navies involved. Consequently the 1930 London Naval Treaty introduced the concept of Type A (heavy) cruisers armed with 8in guns and Type B (light) cruisers with 6in (152mm) guns or smaller, although both types could still displace up to 10,000 tons. Overall tonnage limitations on both types forced the Japanese and American navies to build large Type B cruisers (Mogami and Brooklyn classes) when they would rather have built more Type A. The second London Naval Treaty in 1936 restricted Type B cruisers to 8,000 tons, although only the British, with the Fiji class, took any notice.

In the meantime, however, there was a trend by some navies to produce cruisers whose main function was in the air defence role. The Royal Navy began this by converting some old C class cruisers and then produced the excellent Dido class armed with 10 5.25in (133mm) DP guns, while the US Navy followed suit with the Atlanta class armed with 16 5in (127mm) DP guns. In the meantime, the Japanese persisted with large cruisers, even rearming Type B cruisers with 8in guns, and almost all were well in excess of the 10,000-ton treaty limit. Germany built a few unremarkable light cruisers but the Hipper class heavy cruisers were designed very much with disruption of British sea trade in mind and they carried out several forays into the Atlantic in the opening stages of the war.

During World War II there were a number of fascinating cruiser engagements in which air power played little or no part. These included the sinking of the Italian cruiser *Bartolomeo Colleoni* by the Australian light cruiser HMAS *Sydney* in the Mediterranean (*Sydney* herself was later sunk when she allowed herself to be surprised by the German armed merchant raider *Atlantis* in the Indian Ocean). Other cruiser battles included the Battle of the Java Sea in February 1942 where a force of Australian, British, Dutch and American cruisers was comprehensively defeated by Japanese cruisers and destroyers; the Battle of the Komandorski Islands in the northern Pacific where the USS *Salt Lake City* fought off a superior Japanese force; and the Battle of the Barents Sea where the British cruisers HMS *Jamaica* and HMS *Sheffield* fought off a German attempt to destroy an Arctic convoy.

As the Axis surface fleets declined in strength, such engagements became rarer and the cruiser was mainly utilised as a fleet escort to help protect the aircraft carriers which were the centre of task forces, and to support amphibious operations where their significant firepower was of great assistance to the troops landing and fighting ashore. This was reflected in the alterations made to these ships which generally included removal of aircraft facilities, fitting of extensive arrays of radar and electronic equipment, and substantial increases in short-range AA armament, in some cases requiring the removal of some of the main armament.

County

A late wartime view of HMS Devonshire *showing substantial additions to the light AA armament. (Sydney Goodman Collection)*

HMS Suffolk *in 1940 showing the hangar erected aft, and a cut-down quarterdeck. Cumberland was similarly modified. (Sydney Goodman Collection)*

Britain built a total of 11 10,000-ton 8in (203mm) gun cruisers together with two more for the Royal Australian Navy. Due to the naming policy they were collectively referred to as the County class, although in fact there were three distinct groups.

The first group of five ships was the Kent class laid down in 1926, with a further two for the RAN in the following year. The design was rather conservative by later standards but the ships had a handsome appearance with the main armament disposed symmetrically fore and aft and three raked funnels amidships, the whole carried on a roomy hull with high freeboard. The conventional design left only small margin for protection if the 10,000-ton treaty limit was not to be exceeded and these ships were relatively lightly armoured compared with later foreign designs. However, they were good seaboats and capable of fighting their full armament in almost any weather. The 8in guns were capable of elevation to 70 degrees for AA barrage fire, although in practice this was difficult to achieve.

The next sub-group of four vessels was the London class, laid down in 1926–7, which differed principally in that they adopted an internal system of torpedo protection instead of the amidships hull bulges of the Kents. The bridge and funnels were moved slightly aft to reduce the effects of blast from the forward guns and there were improvements to internal accommodation. Finally, ships of the Dorsetshire class were laid down in 1928–9 and these were similar to the London class except that there were some alterations to the positioning of the secondary armament, and the height of the bridge and after superstructures was reduced.

In the 1930s all were modernised to some extent, the main change being that the secondary armament was increased from four single 4in (102mm) guns to eight 4in guns in twin mountings, and a quadruple 2pdr AA mounting was installed on either beam abreast the funnels. Armour protection was increased and fire control arrangements improved. On *Cumberland* and *Suffolk* the after superstructure was considerably enlarged to incorporate

a large hangar, and a fixed athwartships catapult was fitted so that up to three aircraft could be operated. The quarterdeck aft was cut down as compensation for the increased weight. A much more ambitious modernisation was undertaken with HMS *London* between 1938 and 1941 when she was completely rebuilt so that her appearance was similar to the Fiji class light cruisers.

The County class cruisers were deployed in every theatre of the war and inevitably there were losses. *Cornwall* and *Dorsetshire* were sunk by Japanese aircraft off Ceylon (Sri Lanka) in April 1942, while one of the RAN vessels, *Canberra*, was torpedoed and sunk off Savo Island in a calamitous action in which several USN cruisers were also lost.

SPECIFICATION

Class: County (heavy cruiser) Data *Suffolk* 1941
Displacement: 10,800 tons (14,550 tons full load)
Length: 590ft (179.8m) pp, 630ft (192mm) oa
Beam: 61ft (18.6m) (hull), 68.5ft (20.9m) (over bulges)
Draught: 21ft (6.4m) full load
Machinery: 8 boilers, Parsons SR geared turbines, 4 shafts, 80,000shp
Speed: 31.5kt
Range: 10,400nm (19,260m) at 14kt
Complement: 784
Protection: Main belt 1in (25mm) except 4.5in (114mm) amidships, bulkheads 1in (25mm), decks 1.4in (36mm) (2.5in/64mm over fore and aft citadels). Turret 2in (51mm) (face and tops) and 1.5in (38mm) (sides/rear). Barbettes 1in (25mm). External bulges.
Armament: 8 8in/203mm (4 × 2), 8 4in/102mm AA (4 × 2), 8 2pdr AA (2 × 4), 8 0.5in/13mm AA (2 × 4)
Aircraft: 3. Fixed athwartships catapult abaft funnels.
Ships in Class: *Kent*, *Berwick*, *Cornwall*, *Cumberland*, *Suffolk* (1926); *Australia*, *Canberra* (1927); *Devonshire*, *London* (1927); *Shropshire*, *Sussex* (1928). *Norfolk* (1928); *Dorsetshire* (1929)

HMS Exeter *as refitted following the Battle of the River Plate.* (Sydney Goodman Collection)

With the Washington Treaty setting an overall limit on the total tonnage available for cruisers, it was desirable to reduce the displacement of individual vessels so that more could be built. This reasoning resulted in the laying down of the two ships of the York class in 1927–8 and these were basically diminutives of the County class in which one 8in (203mm) turret was removed and the torpedo armament slightly reduced so that the final displacement was 8,250 tons. As completed, *York* had an aircraft catapult abaft the two raked funnels, plans to fit a second catapult atop B turret having been abandoned, although this accounted for the height of the bridge superstructure. *Exeter* differed in a number of significant respects. As the forward catapult had been abandoned, the opportunity was taken to construct a much more compact and lower bridge structure and the funnels were upright and not raked. Modifications prior to the outbreak of war mainly related to improving the aircraft handling arrangements and the fitting of quadruple 0.5in (13mm) machine gun AA mountings.

HMS *York* took part in the Norwegian campaign before moving to the Mediterranean where she was sunk by Italian explosive motor boats in Suda Bay, Crete, in March 1941. HMS *Exeter* was famously involved in the Battle of the River Plate which resulted in the scuttling of the German pocket battleship *Graf Spee*. However, *Exeter* herself was seriously damaged and on returning to Plymouth she underwent a major reconstruction in which the secondary armament was increased from four to eight 4in (102mm) AA and two eight-barrelled 2pdr AA mountings were fitted. The bridge was enlarged and additional gunnery directors and radar were fitted. In this guise she was sent to the Far East, where in February 1942 she was involved in the Battle of the Java Sea, during which she sustained some damage. Subsequently she was intercepted by Japanese heavy cruisers and sunk by a combination of gunfire and torpedoes on 1 March 1942.

SPECIFICATION

Class: Exeter (heavy cruiser) Data *Exeter* as completed 1931
Displacement: 8,390 tons (10,500 tons full load)
Length: 540ft (164.6m) pp, 575ft (175.3m) oa
Beam: 58ft (17.7m)
Draught: 20.5ft (6.2m) full load
Machinery: 8 boilers, Parsons SR geared turbines, 4 shafts, 80,000shp
Speed: 32kt
Range: 10,000nm (18,250km) at 14kt
Complement: 630 (peacetime)
Protection: Main belt 3in (76mm), bulkheads 1in (25mm), decks 1.5–2.5in (38–64mm). Turrets 2in (51mm) (faces) and 1.5in (38mm) (sides). Barbettes 1in (25mm).
Armament: Guns: 6 8in/203mm (3 × 2), 4 4in/102mm AA (4 × 1), 2 2pdr AA (2 × 1). Torpedoes: 6 21in (533mm) torpedo tubes (2 × 3).
Aircraft: 1. Catapult abaft funnels.
Ships in Class: York (1928), Exeter (1929)

C class cruiser HMS Carlisle *as modified for the AA role.* (Sydney Goodman Collection)

In the 1930s the Royal Navy possessed a significant number of cruisers dating from around the end of World War I. Lacking the sophistication of later ships, they were mostly used for trade protection duties and were not considered suitable for major fleet operations. Nevertheless, they did contribute to the overall numbers of sorely needed cruisers.

The oldest and smallest of these were the 13 C class vessels, originally armed with five 6in (152mm) guns, and in the mid-1930s plans were drawn up to convert these to anti-aircraft escort vessels. *Coventry* and *Curlew* were subsequently rebuilt in 1935–6 and recommissioned with an armament of 10 single 4in (102mm) AA guns controlled by two HA directors, together with two eight-barrelled 2pdr AA mountings. For its time this was a formidable AA armament, and these ships proved their worth when war broke out, being among the small number of RN ships with an effective AA capability.

The success of these conversions led to others, but in order to speed up the process and reduce costs, later vessels received only eight 4in in four twin mountings and one of the multiple 2pdr mountings was omitted. *Curacao, Caledon* (only three twin 4in fitted), *Cairo, Calcutta, Carlisle* and *Colombo* were all converted, although some were not completed until 1942. *Calypso, Cairo, Calcutta* and *Carlisle* were all lost to enemy action while *Curacao* was sunk in a collision with the liner *Queen Mary* in October 1942.

The C class were followed by eight D class cruisers completed 1918–22. Some 20ft (6.1m) longer with increased sheer to the bow, they mounted an additional 6in gun and extra torpedo tubes but were otherwise very similar to their predecessors. Unlike the C class they were not substantially modified and were utilised on second-line duties for most of the war, although *Delhi* was rearmed with five US pattern 5in/38cal guns during a refit in America in 1941–2. *Dunedin* was torpedoed and sunk in November 1944 while *Dragon* and *Durban* were scuttled off Normandy in June 1944 to form part of a breakwater protecting the Mulberry harbours. There were also two 7,500-ton Emerald class cruisers completed in 1926 which were basically enlarged and faster D class, and also three 10,000-ton Hawkins class cruisers of which two were armed with 7.5in (190mm) guns, and a third (*Effingham*) had been rearmed with nine 6in guns although was lost off Norway in 1940 after striking a rock.

D class cruiser HMS Delhi *was uniquely armed with US pattern 5in (127mm) guns during a refit, 1941–2.* (Sydney Goodman Collection)

SPECIFICATION

Class: C and D Classes (light cruiser) Data *Cairo* as AA ship 1939
Displacement: 4,290 tons (5,250 tons full load)
Length: 425ft (129.5m) pp, 451.5ft (137.6m) oa
Beam: 43.5ft (13.3m)
Draught: 15.5ft (4.7m) full load
Machinery: 6 boilers, Brown-Curtiss SR geared turbines, 2 shafts, 40,000shp
Speed: 29kt
Range: 5,900nm (10,930km) at 10kt
Complement: 400+
Protection: Main belt 1.5–3in (38–76mm), decks 1in (25mm)
Armament: 8 4in/102mm AA (4 × 2), 4 2pdr AA (1 × 4), 8 0.5in/13mm AA (2 × 4)
Aircraft: nil
Ships in Class: *Caledon, Calypso, Caradoc* (1916–7); *Cardiff, Ceres, Coventry, Curacao, Curlew* (1917); *Cairo, Capetown, Calcutta, Carlisle, Colombo* (1918–9); *Danae, Dauntless, Delhi, Despatch, Diomede, Dragon, Dunedin, Durban* (1918–19)

HMS Orion *survived the war despite being heavily damaged off Crete in 1941.* (Sydney Goodman Collection)

With worldwide commitments (the British merchant navy was far and away the largest in the world between the two wars), the Royal Navy had an obvious requirement for large numbers of cruisers. In fact the figure was provisionally set at 70, but it was obvious that these could not all be 10,000-ton heavy cruisers both because of treaty limitations and simple economic forces. The Admiralty therefore proposed a class of 6,500-ton light cruisers armed with 6in (152mm) guns which was much more suited to British needs than the larger vessels. The first was ordered in 1929 and a total of five were eventually commissioned as the Leander class. As completed they were over the self-imposed 6,500-ton target but apart from the main armament of eight 6in guns, they were otherwise similarly armed to the County class and represented excellent value for money. The attributes of the design were recognised by the RAN who took over a further three vessels (Sydney class) which were built to a modified design in which the unit machinery system was adopted so that these ships had two well-spaced funnels instead of the single broad-trunked funnel of the Royal Navy Leanders.

Of the RN vessels, *Ajax* and *Achilles* were involved in the Battle of the River Plate, and while the former had an active war in Europe and the Mediterranean, *Achilles* served in the Pacific with the New Zealand Division. *Neptune* was lost after straying into an Italian minefield while serving with the highly successful Force K in the Mediterranean in December 1941. The Australian vessels were heavily engaged in the Pacific where the *Sydney* was lost in a surprise encounter with a German auxiliary cruiser on 19 November 1941. *Perth* was overwhelmed by Japanese forces on 1 March 1942 in the aftermath of the Battle of the Java Sea, leaving only *Hobart*, which had a hectic war in the Pacific and was seriously damaged when torpedoed by a Japanese submarine in July 1943. She was not ready for service again until early 1945, and was finally scrapped in 1962.

HMS Achilles *served with the RN New Zealand Division until 1943. After the war, in 1948, she was transferred to the RIN and renamed Delhi. Note that X turret has been removed in order to mount additional 40mm (1.6in) guns.* (Author's Collection)

SPECIFICATION

Class: Leander/Perth (light cruiser) Data *Leander* 1939
Displacement: 7,270 tons (8,950 tons full load)
Length: 522ft (159.1m) pp, 554.5ft (169m) oa
Beam: 55ft (16.8m)
Draught: 19ft (5.8m) (mean)
Machinery: 6 boilers, Parsons SR geared turbines, 4 shafts, 72,000shp
Speed: 32kt
Range: 5,730nm (10,610km) at 13kt
Complement: 570 (peacetime)
Protection: Main belt 4in (102mm), bulkheads 1.5in (38mm), decks 1.25in (32mm) (2in/51mm over magazines). Turrets 1in (25mm). Barbettes 1in (25mm).
Armament: Guns: 8 6in/152mm (4 × 2), 8 4in/102mm AA (4 × 2), 12 0.5in/13mm AA (3 × 4). Torpedoes: 8 21in (533mm) torpedo tubes (2 × 4).
Aircraft: 1. One catapult abaft funnel.
Ships in Class: Leander (1931); Orion, Achilles (1932); Neptune (1933); Ajax (1934); Perth, Sydney, Hobart (1934)

Arethusa

Arethusa class light cruiser HMS **Penelope.** *(Sydney Goodman Collection)*

The ongoing trend in reducing the size and cost of British cruisers resulted in the 5,500-ton Arethusa class laid down in 1933–5. Their prime role was envisaged as trade protection with the particular task of countering German armed merchant cruisers. Consequently a main armament of only six 6in (152mm) guns was accepted, although in every other respect they were the equal of larger cruisers. Changes of policy resulted in only four being ordered and these were all completed by 1937. All except *Aurora* were completed with a catapult for a Hawker Osprey or Fairey Seafox. However, aircraft facilities were removed during the war so that the close-range AA armament could be increased. Already by 1939 all except *Arethusa* carried a secondary armament of eight 4in (102mm) AA guns, and she followed suit in a 1942 refit, while all vessels had their light AA armament supplemented by the addition of quadruple 2pdr AA mountings.

Despite their small size, these ships were regarded as fleet cruisers and were used as such. *Arethusa* took part in the Oran action, the *Bismarck* operation and the Malta convoys before being torpedoed in November 1942. After repairs in America she supported the Normandy landings. *Aurora* initially operated with the Home Fleet but then spent much of the war in the Mediterranean before being sold to China in 1948 and scrapped in 1955. *Galatea* was torpedoed and sunk off Alexandria on 14 December 1941, and *Penelope*, after a distinguished career in the Mediterranean, was torpedoed and sunk by the German submarine *U-410* while supporting the Anzio landings in February 1944.

SPECIFICATION

Class: Arethusa (light cruiser) Data *Arethusa* 1939
Displacement: 5,220 tons (6,665 tons full load)
Length: 480ft (146.3m) pp, 506ft (154.2m) oa
Beam: 51ft (15.5m)
Draught: 17ft (5.2m) full load
Machinery: 4 boilers, Parsons SR geared turbines, 4 shafts, 64,000shp
Speed: 32kt
Range: 5,300nm (9,815km) at 13kt
Complement: 500 (peacetime)
Protection: Main belt 2.75in (70mm), bulkheads 1in (25mm), decks 1in (25mm) (2in/51mm over magazines and other vital compartments). Turrets 1in (25mm), Barbettes 0.75in (19mm).
Armament: Guns: 6 6in/152mm (3 × 2), 8 4in/102mm AA (4 × 2), 8 0.5in/13mm AA (2 × 4). Torpedoes: 6 21in (533m) torpedo tubes (2 × 3).
Aircraft: 1. One catapult between the funnels.
Ships in Class: *Arethusa, Galatea* (1934); *Penelope* (1935); *Aurora* (1936)

HMS **Arethusa** *as completed. At this time the secondary armament comprised four single 4in (102mm) guns abreast the after funnel, but this was increased to four twin mountings before 1939.* *(Wright & Logan Collection)*

Southampton

A photo of HMS Birmingham *showing the distinctive outline of this class with two raked funnels and a large hangar incorporated abaft the bridge.* (Sydney Goodman Collection)

The Royal Navy was forced to reconsider its policy of building small cruisers when details of the Japanese Mogami class were revealed. Their armament of 15 6in (152mm) guns would quickly overwhelm smaller ships and the United States had already reacted with the decision to build the 10,000-ton Brooklyn class (cf). The British response did not go to the extremes of the US and Japanese designs, instead producing a well-balanced cruiser with an armament of 12 6in guns in four triple turrets equally disposed fore and aft on a displacement of just over 9,000 tons. A large aircraft hangar was integrated into the rear of the bridge superstructure and a fixed athwartships catapult installed between the two raked funnels. AA armament included four twin 4in (102mm) mountings controlled by two HA directors and multiple 2pdr mountings high up on the hangar roof where they commanded excellent arcs of fire. Eight ships of the resulting Southampton class were laid down between 1934 and 1936 and all were completed before the outbreak of war. Interestingly, in 1938 HMS *Sheffield* was the first British warship to be fitted with radar. War modifications to the class included substantial increases in the light AA armament, removal of aircraft facilities, and the addition of various radars. Towards the end of the war, most of the surviving vessels had X turret removed so as to provide yet more space for additional 2pdr and 40mm (1.6in) AA guns to counter kamikaze tactics in the Pacific.

The first war loss was *Southampton*, hit by bombs on 11 January 1941 while involved in Malta convoy operations. *Gloucester* was also lost to air attack on 22 May 1941 off Crete, and *Manchester* was torpedoed by Italian MTBs off Tunisia in August 1942. *Liverpool* was torpedoed and seriously damaged in June 1942 during Operation Harpoon (a Malta convoy) and did not recommission until October 1945. Two further vessels, *Edinburgh* and *Belfast*, were laid down in 1936 to a modified design in which the hull was lengthened and a pair of twin 4in AA mountings was added. Due to an internal rearrangement of the magazines, the funnels were repositioned further aft and the aircraft catapult was now positioned in a gap between the hangar and the fore funnel. Both were completed in 1939, but *Edinburgh* was lost while covering a Russian convoy in May 1942. *Belfast* was seriously damaged by a mine in November 1939 and was out of action until the end of 1942. Subsequently she was involved in the sinking of the *Scharnhorst* in December 1943 and was the flagship of the Eastern Task Force during the Normandy landings in June 1944.

SPECIFICATION

Class: Southampton (light cruiser) Data *Sheffield* 1941
Displacement: 9,100 tons (11,350 tons full load)
Length: 558ft (170.1m) pp, 591.5ft (180.3m) oa
Beam: 62ft (18.9m)
Draught: 20ft (6.1m) full load
Machinery: 4 3-drum boilers, Parsons SR geared turbines, 4 shafts, 75,000shp
Speed: 32kt
Range: 7,700nm (14,260km) at 13kt
Complement: 930
Protection: Main belt 4.5in (114mm), bulkheads 2.5in (64mm), decks 1.5in (38mm) (2–4in/51–102mm over magazines). Turrets 1–2in (25–51mm). Barbettes 1in (25mm).
Armament: Guns: 12 6in/152mm (4 × 3), 8 4in/102mm AA (4 × 2), 8 2pdr AA (2 × 4), six 20mm/0.8in AA (6 × 1). Torpedoes: 6 21in (533mm) torpedo tubes (2 × 3).
Aircraft: 2. One fixed athwartships catapult.
Ships in Class: Southampton, Newcastle, Glasgow, Sheffield, Birmingham (1936); Liverpool, Manchester, Gloucester (1937); Belfast, Edinburgh (1938)

HMS Belfast *in 1942 after completing repairs following major damage by a mine in 1939.* (Sydney Goodman Collection)

HMS **Jamaica** *in 1945 with X turret removed.* (Sydney Goodman Collection)

The 1937 London Navy Treaty set a limit of 8,000 tons on individual cruisers and this precluded the construction of further examples of the Southampton class. Although a number of alternative sketch designs were considered, the outcome was basically a shortened version of the earlier class with a reduction in armour protection, a reduced light AA armament and no torpedo tubes in order to save weight. A transom stern was adopted, partly to compensate for the reduction in hull length, but it did have benefits in providing additional accommodation space. Eleven ships were laid down in 1938–9 but building delays, partly as a result of enemy action, meant that the last three were completed to a modified design in which X turret was removed and replaced by a quadruple 2pdr AA mounting, and in fact this modification was applied to most of the remaining vessels later in the war. With the outbreak of war in 1939, the 8,000-ton treaty limit was disregarded and subsequently all vessels shipped the torpedo armament, and the light AA armament was considerably enhanced. Radar equipment was fitted as it became available.

Despite their relatively small size, these were highly successful ships and were much in demand. *Fiji* was an early war loss, sunk off Crete in May 1941, and *Trinidad* was lost in May 1942 while escorting a Russian convoy. *Uganda* was hit and damaged by a glider bomb off Salerno in September 1943 and proceeded to the United States for repair, after which she was transferred to the Royal Canadian Navy for service in the Pacific.

A further group of cruisers was laid down in 1941–2 as the Minotaur class but only one of these, *Swiftsure*, was completed in time to see service before the end of hostilities. They were basically repeats of the Modified Fiji class except that a twin 4in (102mm) AA replaced the 2pdr mounting in X position.

HMS **Trinidad** *as completed in 1941. Note the gunnery control position atop X turret.* (Sydney Goodman Collection)

SPECIFICATION

Class: Fiji (light cruiser) Data *Nigeria* 1945
Displacement: 9,400 tons (11,200 tons full load)
Length: 538ft (164m) pp, 555.5ft (169.3m) oa
Beam: 62ft (18.9m)
Draught: 22ft (6.7m) full load
Machinery: 4 3-drum boilers, Parsons SR geared turbines, 4 shafts, 72,500shp
Speed: 32kt
Range: 6,520nm (12,075km) at 13kt
Complement: 920
Protection: Main belt 3.5in (89mm), bulkheads 2in (51mm), decks 2in (51mm) (max). Turrets 1–2in (25–51mm). Barbettes 1in (25mm).
Armament: Guns: 12 6in/152mm (4 × 3), 8 4in/102mm AA (4 × 2), 8 2pdr AA (2 × 4), 18 20mm/0.8in AA (8 × 2, 2 × 1). Torpedoes: 6 21in (533mm) torpedo tubes (2 × 3).
Aircraft: 2. One athwartships catapult (all removed 1944).
Ships in Class: *Fiji, Kenya, Mauritius, Nigeria* (1939); *Trinidad, Gambia, Jamaica* (1940); *Uganda, Bermuda, Newfoundland* (1941); *Ceylon* (1942)

Dido

Post-war view of HMS Cleopatra *showing Q turret replaced by a multiple 40mm (1.6in) AA mounting.* (Author's Collection)

While the Royal Navy was forced to build large cruisers to counter the Japanese ships, by 1935 Britain was awakening to the need to rearm and there was an urgent need to expand the cruiser force to some 70 ships. Construction of smaller cruisers would help to increase the numbers available and the existing Arethusa class formed a good basis for a new design. However, instead of arming the ships with 10 guns of mixed 6in (152mm) and 4in (102mm) calibre, it was decided to standardise on the new 5.25in (133mm) dual-purpose gun which was also being produced as the secondary armament for the new King George V class battleships. These were disposed in five twin mountings, three forward and two aft, and were controlled by two HA directors in the AA role and a single DCT for surface gunnery. Two quadruple 2pdr AA and two triple 21in (533mm) torpedo tube mountings completed the armament, but there was no provision for aircraft operation.

Eleven Dido class were laid down 1937–9 and these entered service from 1940 onwards, followed by a further five modified Dido class in which the third forward 5.25in mounting was replaced by a multiple 2pdr AA, the bridge structure was of a lower profile and the masts and funnels were upright instead of being raked aft as in the earlier

group. Due to a bottleneck in the production of the 5.25in mounting, some of the first group were initially completed with only four mountings while *Charybdis* and *Scylla* were given a temporary armament of eight 4.5in (114mm) DP guns in four twin mountings.

Most of the class were utilised in the Mediterranean where their heavy AA fire made them invaluable. Only one was actually lost to air attack: HMS *Spartan*, hit by a German guided bomb off the Anzio beachhead in January 1944. However, *Bonaventure*, *Naiad*, *Hermione* and *Charybdis* were all lost to submarine torpedo attacks. *Argonaut* nearly went the same way, losing her bow and stern to two torpedo hits in December 1942, but was eventually able to proceed to America for repairs.

SPECIFICATION

Class: Dido (light cruiser AA) Data *Euryalus* as completed 1941
Displacement: 5,600 tons (6,850 tons full load)
Length: 485ft (147.8m) pp, 512ft (156.1m) oa
Beam: 50.5ft (15.4m)
Draught: 17.5ft (5.3m) full load
Machinery: 4 boilers, Parsons SR geared turbines, 4 shafts, 62,000shp
Speed: 32kt
Range: 4,850nm (8,980km) at 11kt
Complement: 530
Protection: Main belt 3in (76mm), bulkheads 1in (25mm), decks 1in (25mm) (2in/51mm over magazines). Turrets 1.5in (38mm) (faces) and 1in (25mm) (sides and crowns). Barbettes 0.75in (19mm).
Armament: Guns: 10 5.25in/133mm DP (5 × 2), 8 2pdr AA (2 × 4), 8 0.5in/13mm AA (2 × 4). Torpedoes: 6 21in (533mm) torpedo tubes (2 × 3).
Aircraft: nil
Ships in Class: *Bonaventure, Naiad, Phoebe, Dido, Euryalus, Hermione* (1939); *Sirius, Cleopatra, Charybdis, Scylla* (1940); *Argonaut* (1941); *Spartan, Bellona, Black Prince, Royalist, Diadem* (1942)

HMS Charybdis *was completed with a main armament of 4.5in (114mm) guns due to a shortage of the intended 5.25in (133mm) mountings.* (Sydney Goodman Collection)

USS Indianapolis *(CA 35) as completed in 1932. (Author's Collection)*

American heavy cruiser construction began in the late 1920s when the two ships of the Pensacola class were laid down. These were armed with 10 8in (203mm) guns unusually arranged with a triple turret overfiring the lower twin turret fore and aft. A unit machinery arrangement was adopted for better damage control and this resulted in two widely spaced raked funnels. A distinctive feature of these ships was the flush-decked hull, but the succeeding Northampton class had a raised forecastle for improved seaworthiness and the main armament was altered to nine 8in guns in three triple turrets. The weight saved by this arrangement was used to improve armour protection, but both classes remained well within the 10,000-ton treaty limit. The two Portland class vessels completed in 1932–3 had further improvements to the armour protection in a deliberate attempt to ensure that the tonnage shortfall was eliminated. All three classes featured prominent tripod fore and main masts, and while the Pensacola and Northampton classes originally shipped torpedo tubes, these were removed in 1935. During World War II the light AA armament was substantially increased in all ships, fire control arrangements were improved and radar equipment was added.

Cruisers proved to be indispensable in the Pacific war, and these ships were heavily engaged. *Salt Lake City* and *Pensacola* survived the war but several Northampton class were lost in action including the

nameship which was torpedoed by a Japanese destroyer off Savo Island and sank on 1 December 1942. *Houston* was sunk by the Japanese heavy cruisers *Mikuma* and *Mogami* after the Battle of the Java Sea (March 1942) while *Chicago* was torpedoed in an aircraft attack off Rennell Island on 29 January 1943. *Portland* survived an aircraft torpedo attack in October 1942 and was also damaged off Guadalcanal but was repaired and survived the war. Perhaps the most tragic loss was *Indianapolis*, which was torpedoed by a Japanese submarine on 29 July 1945 while en route to Leyte after delivering the first atomic bomb to Tinian. The loss of life as a result of the torpedo was macabrely increased over the next few days as many survivors died in the shark-infested waters while awaiting a rescue which was delayed due to faulty reporting procedures.

Northampton class heavy cruiser USS Augusta *(CA 31) as she appeared in 1945. Note the raked funnel caps. (Wright & Logan Collection)*

SPECIFICATION

Class: Pensacola/Northampton/Portland (heavy cruiser)
Data *Northampton* 1942
Displacement: 9,050 tons (12,150 tons full load)
Length: 569ft (173.4m) wl, 600.5ft (183m) oa
Beam: 66ft (20.1m)
Draught: 24ft (7.3m) full load
Machinery: 8 boilers, Parsons geared turbines, 4 shafts, 107,000shp
Speed: 32.5kt
Range: 10,000nm (18,250km) at 15kt
Complement: c. 1,100
Protection: Main belt 3in (76mm), bulkheads 2–3in (51–76mm), decks 1–2in (25–51mm). Turrets 1.5–2.25in (38–57mm). Barbettes 1.5in (38mm).
Armament: 9 8in/203mm (3 x 3), 8 5in/127mm AA (8 x 1), 16 1.1in/28mm AA (4 x 4), 14 20mm/0.8in AA (14 x 1)
Aircraft: 4. Two catapults.
Ships in Class: *Pensacola, Salt Lake City* (1929); *Northampton, Chester, Houston* (1929); *Louisville, Chicago, Augusta* (1930); *Indianapolis* (1931); *Portland* (1932)

New Orleans class heavy cruiser USS Tuscaloosa (CA 37). *Note floatplanes on catapults abaft the funnels. (Sydney Goodman Collection)*

The New Orleans class were again built right up to the maximum treaty tonnage of 10,000 tons and were evolved from the preceding Portland class with which they shared the same main armament of nine 8in (203mm) guns in three triple turrets. However, a rearrangement of the machinery spaces allowed a slight decrease in length and the two funnels were closer together, while the forecastle deck was further extended to abreast the after funnel. The aircraft catapults were moved to abaft the funnels and up to four aircraft could be housed in a large hangar built into the after superstructure. The previous heavy tripod masts were replaced by lighter polemasts. The weight saved by shortening the hull was utilised to improve armour protection, and the main belt was increased in size and thickness while the turrets and barbettes were also reinforced. War modifications were limited due to stability problems and consisted mainly of the addition of light AA guns and radar equipment, although in some ships one crane and a catapult were removed to compensate.

Astoria, *Quincy* and *Vincennes* were all sunk on the night of 8 August 1942 in the Battle of Savo Island, a major defeat for the US Navy. However, the remaining vessels survived the war. *Wichita*, the eighth ship of the class, was completed in 1939 to a modified design based on the Brooklyn class light cruisers but mounting nine 8in guns in triple turrets. This featured a full-length flush-decked hull with a high freeboard. Aircraft handling arrangements were concentrated at the stern allowing a tidier superstructure which in turn permitted a more efficient deployment of the secondary armament, which consisted of eight single 5in/38cal (127mm) DP guns.

The cruiser USS Wichita (CA 45) *was the sole example of this type, the design of which was based on the Brooklyn class light cruisers. (Sydney Goodman Collection)*

SPECIFICATION

Class: New Orleans/Wichita (heavy cruiser) Data *Astoria* 1941
Displacement: 9,950 tons (13,500 tons full load)
Length: 574ft (175m) wl, 588ft (179.2m) oa
Beam: 61.75ft (18.8m)
Draught: 25ft (7.6m)
Machinery: 8 boilers, Westinghouse geared turbines, 4 shafts, 107,000shp
Speed: 32.75kt
Range: 10,000nm (18,250km) at 15kt
Complement: c. 1,100
Protection: Main belt 1.5–5in (38–127mm), bulkheads 5in (127mm), decks 0.5–3in (13–76mm). Turrets 3–5in (76–127mm). Barbettes 5in (127mm).
Armament: 9 8in/203mm (3 × 3), 8 5in/127mm AA (8 × 1), 16 1.1in/28mm AA (4 × 4)
Aircraft: 4. Two catapults abaft the funnels.
Ships in Class: *New Orleans, San Francisco, Minneapolis, Tuscaloosa, Astoria* (1933); *Quincy* (1935); *Vincennes* (1936); *Wichita* (1937)

Heavy cruiser USS New Orleans *(CA 32). (Author's Collection)*

Baltimore class heavy cruiser USS Chicago *(CA 136). (Author's Collection)*

By 1940 the US Navy was no longer bound by treaty limitations and was able to resume the building of heavy cruisers. The design was loosely based on the Wichita class but with substantially increased hull dimensions, while the machinery layout owed much to the Cleveland class light cruisers then being built. A main armament of nine 8in (203mm) guns in three triple turrets was retained but the secondary armament was substantially increased to 12 5in/38cal (127mm) guns in six twin turrets. In addition a heavy battery of 40mm (1.6in) and 20mm (0.8in) guns was planned from the outset. Protection was generally to the same standard as the Wichita. Up to four aircraft could be carried although only two could be stowed in the hangar under the quarterdeck. There were no side scuttles or other openings in the hull and all internal spaces were mechanically ventilated and provided with electrical lighting. Freed from the treaty limitations, standard displacement rose to over 13,000 tons and the increased beam much improved stability.

Contracts for the first four ships were placed in mid-1940, although these were not completed until

1943 and some of the later vessels were not commissioned until after the war. These included *Oregon City*, *Albany* and *Rochester*, which were completed to a modified design in which the boiler uptakes were trunked into a single funnel allowing the superstructure to be shortened. Those ships completed in time to see action gave good service, and none was lost to enemy action. At the end of August 1945, some 13 Baltimore class were in commission but some of these had only just been completed and were too late to see action. In many respects the Baltimore class were possibly the best heavy cruiser built by any of the combatant nations as, at the time of their construction, they were able to incorporate many of the lessons learnt in the first years of the war.

SPECIFICATION

Class: Baltimore (heavy cruiser) Data *Baltimore* as completed
Displacement: 13,600 tons (17,070 tons full load)
Length: 664ft (202.4m) wl, 675ft (205.7m) oa
Beam: 71ft (21.6m)
Draught: 26ft (7.9m) full load
Machinery: 4 boilers, General Electric geared turbines, 4 shafts, 120,000shp
Speed: 33kt
Range: 10,000nm (18,250km) at 15kt
Complement: 1,700
Protection: Main belt 6in (152mm), bulkheads 6in (152mm), decks 2–3in (51–76mm). Turrets 3–6in (76–152mm). Barbettes 6in (152mm).
Armament: 9 8in/203mm (3 × 3), 12 5in/127mm DP (6 × 2), 48 40mm/1.6in AA (12 × 4), 24 20mm/0.8in AA (24 × 1)
Aircraft: 4. Two catapults.
Ships in Class: *Baltimore, Boston* (1942); *Canberra, Quincy* (1943); *Pittsburgh, St Paul, Columbus, Bremerton, Fall River, Macon, Los Angeles, Chicago* (1944); *Helena, Toledo* (1945)

A post-war view of USS Baltimore *(CA 68). (Wright & Logan Collection)*

Omaha

Colour photo of USS Concord *(CL 10) taken in 1943.* (US Navy Historical Branch)

The Omaha class of 10 light cruisers were ordered in 1917 when the United States entered World War I and were the first cruisers laid down for the US Navy since the three Chester class of 1905. Their design incorporated much of the wartime experience gained from British and German cruiser operations and it was intended that the US ships should be larger and faster than their contemporaries. The design was cast around a very slim hull with high installed power which necessitated four funnels and a tripod foremast carrying a fighting top which gave these ships a very distinctive appearance. The main armament comprised 12 6in (152mm) guns carried in a twin turret fore and aft and single casemate mountings grouped around the bridge and after superstructure. A heavy torpedo armament was carried and two aircraft were carried on catapults abaft the funnels. As completed, these ships were found to be overweight by more than 400 tons and this had an adverse effect on speed and stability. By the outbreak of World War II, the torpedo armament had been reduced to six tubes, and two of the after single 6in casemate guns were removed in some ships. Although there were plans to convert these ships to anti-aircraft cruisers, along the lines of the British C class cruisers, these were never implemented and war modifications entailed the removal of aircraft and catapults and the addition of several 40mm (1.6in) and 20mm (0.8in) AA guns.

As newer ships came into service they were relegated to second-line duties, although the USS *Marblehead* was one of the few Allied vessels to survive the Battle of the Java Sea in February 1942, despite being seriously damaged by air attack. All survived the war but were scrapped almost immediately at the end of hostilities. *Milwaukee* was loaned to the Russian Navy in 1944 and renamed *Murmansk*. She was returned in 1949 and then broken up.

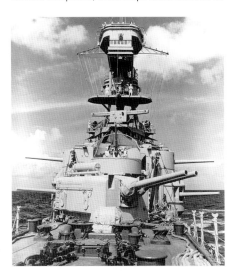

Foredeck of the USS Memphis *(CL 13) showing the forward twin 6in (152mm) turret and the casemate-mounted single 6in guns.* (US Navy Historical Branch)

SPECIFICATION

Class: Omaha (light cruiser) Data *Omaha* 1940
Displacement: 7,050 tons (9,150 tons full load)
Length: 550ft (167.6m) wl, 555.5ft (169.3m) oa
Beam: 55.5ft (16.9m)
Draught: 20ft (6.1m) full load
Machinery: 12 boilers, geared turbines, 4 shafts, 90,000shp
Speed: 34kt
Range: 8,500nm (15,740m) at 10kt
Complement: 800
Protection: Main belt 3in (76mm), bulkheads 2–3in (51–76mm), decks 1.5in (38mm). Turrets and casemates 1–2in (25–51mm). Barbettes 1–2in (25–51mm).
Armament: Guns: 12 6in/152mm (2 × 2, 8 × 1), 4 3in/76mm AA, 2 3pdr, 8 0.5in/13mm AA. Torpedoes: 6 (2 × 3) 21in (533mm) torpedo tubes.
Aircraft: 2. Two catapults abaft funnels.
Ships in Class: *Omaha* (1920); *Milwaukee, Cincinnati, Richmond, Concord* (1921); *Raleigh, Detroit* (1922); *Trenton, Marblehead* (1923); *Memphis* (1924)

Brooklyn class cruiser USS Philadelphia *(CL 41). Note the five triple 6in (152mm) gun turrets.* (Sydney Goodman Collection)

The 1930 London Naval Treaty set overall tonnage limitations for 8in (203mm) armed cruisers and the US Navy would reach their allocated limit with the completion of the projected eight New Orleans class. Although it preferred the concept of the heavy cruiser for Pacific operations, the navy was forced to begin building light cruisers and the design was heavily influenced by the appearance of the Japanese Mogami class which mounted no fewer than 15 6in (152mm) guns. The US Navy had no option but to match these, and the resulting Brooklyn class, laid down from 1934 onwards, were similarly armed.

In some respects these ships were based on the New Orleans class heavy cruisers and utilised the same machinery, although a new flush-decked hull with high freeboard was adopted. For the first time, all aircraft facilities were positioned right aft and this arrangement was subsequently adopted for all new cruisers and battleships. The secondary armament consisted of eight single 5in/25cal (127mm) AA guns equally distributed port and starboard, although the last two ships, *St Louis* and *Helena*, carried eight 5in/38cal DP in four twin mountings. During the war these ships carried an increased light AA armament, and by 1945 some carried up to 28 40mm (1.6in) and 20 20mm (0.8in) guns. Radar was added and the midships boat crane removed, while four ships were fitted with hull bulges which improved stability and increased beam by around 8ft (2.4m).

Savannah was seriously damaged off Salerno by a German FX1400 guided bomb, but was repaired. The only war loss was the USS *Helena* which, although surviving the debacle at Savo Island, was torpedoed and sunk by Japanese destroyers in the Battle of Kula Gulf in July 1943. All the other ships survived the war despite most of them receiving serious damage at one time or another – a tribute to the soundness of the basic design. The USS *Phoenix* was sold to Argentina in 1951 and, as the *General Belgrano*, was sunk by a British submarine during the 1982 Falklands War.

USS Nashville *(CL 43) as completed in 1938.* (Wright & Logan Collection)

SPECIFICATION

Class: Brooklyn (light cruiser) Data *Brooklyn* 1941
Displacement: 9,700 tons (12,700 tons full load)
Length: 600ft (182.9m) wl, 608.5ft (185.5m) oa
Beam: 61.75ft (18.8m)
Draught: 24ft (7.3m) full load
Machinery: 8 boilers, Parsons geared turbines, 4 shafts, 100,000shp
Speed: 33kt
Range: 10,000nm (18,250km) at 15kt
Complement: c. 1,200
Protection: Main belt 1.5–4in (38–102mm), bulkheads 4–5in (102–127mm), decks 3in (76mm) (max). Turrets 3–5in (76–127mm). Barbettes 5in (127mm).
Armament: 15 6in/152mm (5 × 3), 8 5in/127mm AA (8 × 1), 4 3pdr (4 × 1), 8 0.5in/13mm AA (8 × 1)
Aircraft: 4. Two stern catapults.
Ships in Class: *Brooklyn, Philadelphia, Boise* (1936); *Savannah, Nashville, Honolulu* (1937); *Phoenix, St Louis, Helena* (1938)

More Cleveland class cruisers were built than any other type of cruiser. Shown here is USS Dayton *(CL 105), one of the last to be completed.* (Wright & Logan Collection)

The outbreak of war in Europe in 1939 highlighted a critical shortage of cruisers for the US Navy, and in order to expedite the construction of new ships the design was based on the USS *Helena*, one of the last of the Brooklyn class cruisers. To improve stability beam was increased by almost 5ft (1.5m) and one 6in (152mm) triple turret was dropped in favour of additional 5in (127mm) mountings for improved AA fire. Freed from the London Treaty restriction of 8,000 tons, the standard displacement remained similar to that of the Brooklyn class at around 10,000 tons. The final armament comprised 12 6in guns in triple turrets evenly distributed fore and aft together with no fewer than 12 5in/38cal (127mm) DP guns in six twin turrets spread around the superstructure. A unit machinery system was adopted and the boiler uptakes carried to two slim raked funnels. Up to four aircraft could be carried with the catapults, crane and hangar all grouped at the stern.

A massive construction programme started with the laying down of the first ships in 1940, and subsequently orders were placed for 30 ships. Nine of these were completed as aircraft carriers (Independence class, cf), but another nine were ordered as replacements, although in the event two of these were never laid down. Ultimately 26 were actually completed as cruisers although one, USS *Manchester* (CL 83), did not commission until 1946. One other vessel, USS *Galveston* (CL 93), was laid down in 1944 but was not eventually commissioned as a guided missile armed cruiser until 1958.

The first ships joined the US Pacific fleet in late 1942 and thereafter the class played an increasingly important part in all operations. Amazingly none was lost to enemy action and all survived the war.

From 1943 onwards the design was recast with the boiler uptakes trunked into a single broad funnel, the superstructure was reorganised into a more compact unit to improve arcs of fire for the 5in guns, and hangar space aft was reduced so that more messdecks could be provided for an increased complement. This variant was known as the Fargo class and, although a total of nine were laid down, only two were actually completed, both in the post-war period. The Cleveland class proved to be one of the most successful cruiser designs of World War II, and at one stage the British Admiralty gave some thought to building similar ships.

SPECIFICATION

Class: Cleveland (light cruiser) Data *Mobile* as completed 1943
Displacement: 10,000 tons (13,755 tons full load)
Length: 600ft (182.9m) wl, 610ft (185.9m)
Beam: 66.5ft (20.3m)
Draught: 25ft (7.6m) full load
Machinery: 4 boilers, General Electric geared turbines, 4 shafts, 100,000shp
Speed: 33kt
Range: 11,000nm (20,370km) at 15kt
Complement: 1,200+
Protection: Main belt 1.5–5in (38–127mm), bulkheads 5in (127mm), decks 3in (76mm) (max). Turrets 3–5in (76–127mm). Barbettes 5in (127mm).
Armament: 12 6in/152mm (4 × 3), 12 5in/127mm DP (6 × 2), 28 40mm/1.6in AA (4 × 4, 6 × 2), 21 20mm/0.8in AA (21 × 1)
Aircraft: 4. Two stern catapults.
Ships in Class: *Cleveland, Columbia* (1941); *Montpelier, Denver, Santa Fe, Birmingham, Mobile, Miami* (1942); *Vincennes, Pasadena, Biloxi, Houston, Vicksburg, Astoria, Wilkes-Barre* (1943); *Springfield, Topeka, Providence, Duluth, Oklahoma City, Little Rock, Amsterdam, Portsmouth, Atlanta, Dayton* (1944); *Galveston* (1945); *Manchester* (1946)

USS Oakland *(CL 95). Compared to the preceding Atlanta class, the wing 5in (127mm) turrets were deleted and close-range AA armament was increased. (Author's Collection)*

USS Flint *(CL 97) was completed in 1944 and saw action with carrier task forces and at Iwo Jima. (Author's Collection)*

The four ships of the Atlanta class were laid down in 1940 and all had entered service by early 1942. They were intended as fleet scouts and escorts, as well as acting in the destroyer support role, although their multiple 5in (127mm) battery was obviously expected to provide an effective AA defence. In this respect they were very similar in concept to the British Dido class (cf). The 16 5in guns were mounted in eight twin turrets disposed three forward, three aft and one on either beam amidships. Both *Atlanta* and *Juneau* were lost in November 1942 in the fierce naval actions around Guadalcanal, but *San Diego* and *San Juan* both survived the war.

The next four ships, known as the Oakland class, were built to a slightly modified design in which the wing twin 5in mountings were replaced by additional quadruple 40mm (1.6in) AA mountings. Both groups carried torpedoes, the Atlantas with two quadruple and the Oaklands with two triple mountings. *Oakland* and *Reno* were completed in 1943 and the other two in 1944–5. Another three ships of the Juneau class were laid down in 1945–6 but were not completed until after the war and then to a modified design in which the arrangement of the 5in mounts was altered.

SPECIFICATION

Class: Atlanta/Oakland (light cruiser AA) Data *Atlanta* as completed 1941
Displacement: 6,000 tons (8,100 tons full load)
Length: 520ft (158.5m) wl, 541.5ft (165m) oa
Beam: 53.25ft (16.2m)
Draught: 26ft (7.9m) full load
Machinery: 4 boilers, Westinghouse geared turbines, 75,000shp
Speed: 33kt
Range: 8,500nm (15,740km) at 15kt
Complement: 810
Protection: Main belt 3.5in (89mm), bulkheads 2–3in (51–76mm), decks 2in (51mm). Turrets 1.5in (38mm). Barbettes 1.5in (38mm).
Armament: Guns: 16 5in/127mm DP (8 × 2), 12 1.1in/28mm AA (3 × 4), 8 20mm/0.8in AA (8 × 1). Torpedoes: 8 21in (533mm) torpedo tubes (2 × 4).
Aircraft: nil
Ships in Class: *Atlanta, Juneau, San Diego, San Juan* (1941); *Oakland, Reno* (1942); *Flint, Tucson* (1944); *Juneau* (ii), *Spokane* (1945); *Fresno* (1946)

Heavy cruiser **Admiral Hipper,** *as completed.* (Sydney Goodman Collection)

Despite being forbidden under the terms of the Versailles Treaty to build heavy cruisers, Germany nevertheless began planning such vessels in 1934 although the first pair were not laid down until 1935 when Hitler renounced the treaty and announced a German rearmament programme. Although not a signatory of the Washington Treaty, a pretence was maintained that the new ships would comply with the 10,000-ton limitation, although as completed they were substantially in excess of that figure. The two ships superficially resembled the Deutschland class pocket battleships, being of a similar size and having a straight-stem single funnel and towerlike bridge structure. The anti-aircraft battery of 12 4.1in (104mm) AA guns in six stabilised twin mountings controlled by no fewer than four HA directors was the most sophisticated in the world at the time. Heavily armoured in comparison with the British County class, they posed a powerful threat. *Blücher* was completed with a raked bow and funnel cap, modifications later extended to the *Admiral Hipper* which subsequently received additional light AA guns and new radar equipment. *Blücher* was an early war loss, sunk by shore-based torpedoes while attempting to convey German troops to Oslo in April 1940. *Hipper* was involved in the Norwegian campaign and made two cruises into the Atlantic, sinking several merchant ships. She was brought to action and seriously damaged in the Battle of the Barents Sea (December 1942) and saw no further operational service.

Three more similar ships were laid down in 1938–9 but only one, *Prinz Eugen*, was completed,

in 1940, with a raked bow and funnel cap and a rearrangement of the aircraft handling arrangements. She took part in the *Bismarck* action and also the Channel dash in February 1942 when she was hit by a torpedo from a British submarine. Although repaired, she remained in the Baltic, surrendered at Copenhagen in May 1945, and was later expended in American atomic bomb trials.

Her two sister ships had rather mixed fortunes. *Lützow* was ceded to the Russians in 1940 while still building and was not completed by the time Germany invaded Russia. Nevertheless, her guns played a major part in the defence of Leningrad and she did see some post-war service with the Russian Navy. *Seydlitz* was almost complete in 1942 when work was suspended and subsequently it was planned to convert her to an aircraft carrier (rather along the lines of the US Independence class). However, although work began, little was actually achieved and she was scuttled in January 1945.

Prinz Eugen *was completed with a raked clipper bow.* (WZ Bilddienst)

SPECIFICATION

Class: Admiral Hipper (heavy cruiser) Data *Admiral Hipper* 1939
Displacement: 13,900 tons (18,600 tons full load)
Length: 640ft (195.1m) wl, 676ft (206m) oa
Beam: 70ft (21.3m)
Draught: 25ft (7.6m) full load
Machinery: 12 high-pressure boilers, Blohm und Voss/AG Weser geared turbines, 3 shafts, 132,000shp
Speed: 32kt
Range: 6,800nm (12,590km) at 19kt
Complement: 1,600
Protection: Main belt 3.25in (83mm), decks 1.25–2.5in (32–64mm). Turrets 6.5in (165mm). Barbettes 3.75in (95mm). External bulges.
Armament: Guns: 8 8in/203mm (4 × 2), 12 4.1in/104mm AA (6 × 2), 12 37mm/1.45in AA (6 × 2), 4 20mm/0.8in AA (4 × 1). Torpedoes: 12 21in (533m) tubes (4 × 3)
Aircraft: Three. One catapult.
Ships in Class: *Admiral Hipper* (1937), *Blücher* (1937), *Prinz Eugen* (1938), *Seydlitz* and *Lützow* (1939)

Light cruiser **Nürnberg** *as completed in 1935. Note the broad funnel.* (Maritime Photo Library)

In 1926 the three cruisers of the Königsberg class were laid down and, although still subject to the 6,000-ton limit, they managed to mount nine 5.9in guns in three triple mountings, unusually disposed two aft and one forward. The after turrets were also displaced slightly to port and starboard of the centreline. To save weight, the hull was welded and scantlings were kept as light as possible. Unfortunately, the compromises necessary to carry a relatively heavy armament within the displacement limits led to some serious structural weaknesses and poor stability margins which restricted their operational effectiveness. Another innovation was the concept of a mixed machinery installation. As well as standard steam turbines, two diesels were also fitted which could be connected to the shafts by a hydraulic coupling and were used mainly to extend the cruising range. At the time of their construction Germany was not permitted to operate aircraft from ships, but in the 1930s all three were subsequently fitted with a single catapult between the funnels, although *Köln* had hers removed in 1938.

Leipzig was laid down in 1928 and completed in 1931. Superficially she was a repeat of the *Köln* class with the obvious external difference of having her boiler uptakes trunked into a single broad funnel. Internally the machinery arrangements were altered with four MAN diesels coupled to a centre shaft while the steam turbines drove two outer shafts. The main armament was all mounted on the centreline and there were improvements to the type and distribution of armour plating. An aircraft and catapult was fitted forward of the funnel in 1936, but further modifications were limited and she had an unfortunate war record. Torpedoed by a British submarine in December 1939, she suffered serious damage to her machinery which was never fully repaired and she was mainly used as a train-

ing vessel. Her unfortunate record continued when she was accidentally rammed by the heavy cruiser *Prinz Eugen*, and she ended the war as a floating battery in defence of the Baltic ports. Captured by the Allies, she was scuttled in 1946.

The *Nürnberg* was virtually a repeat of the *Leipzig* although she was not laid down until 1933 and then completed in November 1935. The main alteration was in the positioning of the funnel, which was moved forward, and the catapult and aircraft were then mounted abaft. The anti-aircraft armament was boosted from six to eight 3.5in (89mm) guns in four twin mountings. In 1939 she was also hit by a torpedo in the same attack which almost sank the *Leipzig*, but her damage was much less severe, although an extensive refit was required. The aircraft and catapult were removed in 1942, and by 1944 her light AA armament had been increased to two 40mm (1.6in), eight 37mm (1.45in) and 29 20mm (0.8in) guns. Like the other German light cruisers, she was employed extensively on training duties and was laid up at Copenhagen for the last few months of the war. She was subsequently handed over to the Russian Navy and served as the *Admiral Makarov* until the 1950s.

SPECIFICATION

Class: Leipzig/Nürnberg (light cruiser) Data *Nürnberg*
Displacement: 6,980 tons (8,970 tons full load)
Length: 557.5ft (169.9m) pp, 593.75ft (181m) oa
Beam: 53.5ft (16.3m)
Draught: 21ft (6.4m) full load
Machinery: 8 boilers, Parsons geared turbines, 2 shafts, 60,000shp; 8 MAN diesel engines, 1 shaft, 12,400bhp
Speed: 32kt
Range: 2,400nm (4,450km) at 13kt
Complement: 896
Protection: Main belt 2in (51mm), decks 1in (25mm) (maximum). Turrets and barbettes 1.25in (32mm).
Armament: Guns: 9 5.9in/150mm (3 × 3), 8 3.5in/89mm AA (4 × 2), 4 20mm/0.8in AA (4 × 1). Torpedoes: 12 21in (533mm) torpedo tubes (4 × 3).
Aircraft: 2. One catapult amidships.
Ships in Class: *Karlsruhe* (1927), *Königsberg* (1927), *Köln* (1928) *Leipzig* (1929), *Nürnberg* (1934)

Stern view of the light cruiser **Leipzig**. (WZ Bilddienst)

The heavy cruiser Gorizia was the only ship of her class to survive the war. The other three were sunk at Matapan.
(Maritime Photo Library)

This class of four heavy cruisers was based on the preceding Trento class (cf) but armour protection was to be increased at the expense of speed. Great efforts were made to keep the displacement within treaty limits and this was partly achieved by a lighter hull structure and by adopting a two-shaft machinery layout. The resulting weight savings allowed total armour protection to be almost doubled but, ultimately, the final displacement approached almost 12,000 tons. An improved pattern of 8in (203mm) gun was adopted and, as completed, the secondary armament comprised sixteen 3.9in (99mm) AA guns. During the late 1930s, some of the latter were removed to allow the close-range AA armament to be supplemented by two twin 37mm (1.45in) mountings. As with the Trento class, the aircraft were carried in a forecastle hangar and launched by means of a fixed compressed air catapult. Unusually for cruisers of this size, no torpedo armament was shipped.

These sister ships often operated together in wartime operations, and in March 1941 *Pola*, *Zara* and *Fiume* formed the 1st Cruiser Division during the Battle of Matapan when the Italian fleet attempted to disrupt the transport of British troops to Greece. On the afternoon of 28 March, British aircraft managed to score a torpedo hit on the *Pola* which was brought to a standstill. *Zara* and *Fiume* were ordered to stand by her and provide assistance, but during the following night the three cruisers were surprised and sunk by a British force

which included two battleships. The fourth ship, *Gorizia*, was not present at Matapan and saw further action until being taken over by German forces while under repair at La Spezia at the time of the Italian surrender in September 1943. She was later sunk in June 1944 by the same combined Italian and British human torpedo attack which also sank the *Bolzano* (cf).

SPECIFICATION

Class: Zara (heavy cruiser) Data *Zara* 1940
Displacement: 11,680 tons (14,300 tons full load)
Length: 547.5ft (166.9m) pp, 557ft (169.8m) oa
Beam: 63ft (19.2m)
Draught: 20ft (6.1m) (mean)
Machinery: 8 boilers, Parsons SR turbines, 2 shafts, 95,000shp
Speed: 32kt
Range: 5,361nm (9,930km) at 16kt
Complement: 830
Protection: Main belt 6in (152mm), decks 2.75in (70mm). Turrets 6in (152mm) (max).
Armament: 8 8in/203mm (4 × 2), 12 3.9in/99 mm AA (8 × 2), 8 37mm/1.45in AA (4 × 2), 8 0.5in/13mm AA
Aircraft: 2. Single bow catapult.
Ships in Class: *Zara*, *Fiume*, *Gorizia* (1931); *Pola* (1932)

Trento/Bolzano

Trieste **photographed at Toulon in 1933.** (Marius Bar Photo)

For the most part the Italian Navy's operations were restricted to the Mediterranean and consequently they had no particular requirement for long-range cruisers and had previously built few vessels of this type. Nevertheless, Italy did not wish to be outclassed by other nations, particularly France, and therefore joined the race to build 10,000-ton 8in (203mm) gun cruisers when the two Trento class were laid down in 1925. An armament of eight 8in guns, equally disposed fore and aft in twin turrets, was selected, and like most Italian warships they were designed for speed although lacked the radius of action of some foreign contemporaries. However, armour protection was better than the British County class and consequently the final displacement was over the treaty limit by at least some 500 tons, although this was not admitted at the time. The aircraft arrangements were unusual in that the hangar was under the forecastle in front of A turret and aircraft were launched from a fixed bow catapult. Both ships received only minor modifications during the war and *Trento* was torpedoed and sunk by a British submarine on 15 June 1942. *Trieste* was also torpedoed in November 1941 and was out of action for some time. She was eventually sunk by US bombers in April 1943.

Bolzano, the third ship of the class, was laid down in 1930 and differed in a number of respects. Although the main armament remained at eight 8in guns, they were of an improved type (as fitted to the Zara class, cf). The arrangement of the armour plating was altered to give increased protection, and more conventional aircraft handling arrangements included a catapult sited between the funnels. After an active war in which she was damaged on several occasions, she was torpedoed by HMS/M *Unbroken* on 13 August 1942 and was still under repair at the time of the Italian surrender in September 1943. She was subsequently sunk by a combined Italian and British human torpedo attack at La Spezia in June 1944.

SPECIFICATION

Class: Trento/Bolzano (heavy cruiser) Data *Trento* 1942
Displacement: 10,500 tons (13,550 tons full load)
Length: 623ft (189.9m) pp, 646ft (196.9m) oa
Beam: 67.5ft (20.6m)
Draught: 22ft (6.7m) (mean)
Machinery: 12 boilers, Parsons SR turbines, 4 shafts, 150,000shp
Speed: 35kt
Range: 4,160nm (7,700km) at 16kt
Complement: 781
Protection: Main belt 2.75in (70mm), decks 2in (51mm). Turrets 4in (102mm).
Armament: 8 8in/203mm AA (4 × 2), 12 3.9in/99mm AA (6 × 2), 8 37mm/1.45in AA (4 × 2), 4 20mm/0.8in AA (4 × 1), 8 0.5in/13mm AA (4 × 2)
Aircraft: 3. One fixed bow catapult.
Ships in Class: *Trieste* (1928), *Trento* (1929), *Bolzano* (1932)

Duca d'Aosta

Light cruiser Emmanuele Filiberto Duca d'Aosta. *Note the Ro.43 floatplane on the catapult amidships.* (Maritime Photo Library)

Italian light cruiser development between the wars was initially prompted by the appearance of the large French destroyers in the mid-1920s. In order to counter these the da Barbiano class of four 5,000-ton light cruisers armed with eight 6in (152mm) guns was laid down in 1928. In an all-out quest for speed, armour protection was virtually non-existent, and on trials they were quoted as achieving 42kt although this was achieved under very artificial conditions and in war trim they rarely exceeded 35kt. All were sunk in action, the *Bartolomeo Colleoni* by the Australian cruiser HMAS *Sydney* in a classic gun duel. The next group of *Condottieri* were two slightly larger vessels of the Luigi Cadorna class which differed mainly in having a lengthened hull and aircraft arrangements moved to abaft the second funnel. The third group of two ships, Raimondo Montecuccoli class, were laid down in 1931 and were further lengthened while displacement rose by almost 2,000 tons, most of this used to provide a much more realistic scheme of armour protection. An aircraft catapult was located between the two widely spaced funnels.

In 1932–3 the two Duca d'Aosta class were laid down and details of these two ships are given in the adjacent data table. Basically the hull was further lengthened and armour protection again increased to the extent that it accounted for 22% of the standard displacement. Both ships survived the war, *Duca d'Aosta* being ceded to Russia and *di Savoia* to the Hellenic Navy.

The final evolution of the Italian light cruiser was the Garibaldi class of two ships in which the arma-

ment was increased to 10 6in guns, and a change in boiler-room layouts resulted in two closely spaced funnels amidships. Both saw considerable post-war service with the Italian Navy before being decommissioned in the 1960s.

SPECIFICATION

Class: Duca d'Aosta (light cruiser) Data *Aosta* 1939
Displacement: 8,317 tons (10,375 tons full load)
Length: 563.5ft (171.8m) pp, 613ft (186.8m) oa
Beam: 57.5ft (17.5m)
Draught: 20ft (6.1m) (mean)
Machinery: 6 boilers, Parsons geared turbines, 2 shafts, 110,000shp
Speed: 36kt
Range: 3,900nm (7,220km) at 14kt
Complement: c. 700
Protection: Main belt 3in (76mm), decks 1.5in (38mm). Turrets 3.5in (89mm).
Armament: Guns: 8 6in/152mm (4 × 2), 6 3.9in/99mm AA (3 × 2), 8 37mm/1.45in AA (4 × 2), 12 0.5in/13mm AA (6 × 2). Torpedoes: 6 21in (533mm) torpedo tubes (2 × 3). Other: 96 mines in lieu of torpedo tubes.
Aircraft: 2. One catapult amidships.
Ships in Class: *Emanuele Filiberto Duca d'Aosta* (1935), *Eugenio di Savoia* (1936)

Aoba (shown here) and Kinugasa *were completed with 8in (203mm) guns in twin turrets.* (US Navy Historical Branch)

The two Furutaka class cruisers were laid down in 1922 and their design was completed well before the signing of the Washington Treaty which subsequently had the effect of encouraging the building of 10,000-ton cruisers. The two Japanese ships, armed with only six 8in (203mm) guns and utilising new weight-saving construction methods, were well below that figure. Despite this, at 9,000 tons they were well over the original target figure of 7,500 tons. As completed in 1927, the main armament was carried in six single mountings in weatherproof gunhouses. However, in a major refit in the late 1930s, the armament was remounted in three twin turrets, two forward and one aft, and the secondary armament improved from four single 3.1in (79mm) AA guns to four 4.7in (119mm) guns. The hull was given wider bulges to increase stability, which still remained marginal. The change to twin turrets brought these ships into line with the later Aoba class (two ships laid down in 1924) which were basically repeats of the Furutaka except for the armament layout. In their final configuration the two classes could be distinguished by the fact that the Furutakas carried a catapult and aircraft between the after funnel and mainmast, while in the Aoba class it was situated abaft the mainmast.

After the outbreak of war in 1941, all four ships formed the 6th Cruiser Squadron of the Japanese Combined Fleet and took part in several actions including the Battle of Savo Island (August 1942) in which several Allied cruisers were lost. However, *Kako* was torpedoed by a US submarine

as she withdrew and *Furutaka* was sunk at the Battle of Cape Esperance the following October. *Kinugasa* was sunk by American carrier-based aircraft in November 1942, while *Aoba* had been badly damaged at the Battle of Cape Esperance, although she eventually returned to service in late 1943. In October 1944 she was hit by a torpedo from a US submarine, was never repaired, and was eventually sunk at Kure by air attack in mid-1945.

SPECIFICATION

Class: Furutaka/Aoba (heavy cruiser) Data *Aoba* 1939
Displacement: 7,100 tons (8,900 tons full load)
Length: 585ft (178.3m) pp, 607.5ft (185.2m) oa
Beam: 52ft (15.8m)
Draught: 18.5ft (5.6m) (mean)
Machinery: 12 Kanpon boilers, geared turbines, 4 shafts, 102,000shp
Speed: 34.5kt
Range: 6,000nm (11,110km) at 14kt
Complement: c. 770
Protection: Main belt 3in (76mm), decks 1.4in (36mm), magazines 2in (51mm). Turrets 1in (25mm).
Armament: Guns: 6 8in/203mm (3 × 2), 4 4.7in/119mm AA (4 × 1), 8 25mm/1in AA (4 × 2), 4 0.5in/13mm AA (2 × 2). Torpedoes: 8 24in (610mm) torpedo tubes (2 × 4).
Aircraft: 2. One catapult.
Ships in Class: *Furutaka, Kako* (1925); *Aoba, Kinugasa* (1926)

Myoko was the first of a class of four 10,000-ton heavy cruisers. Note the unusual disposition of the forward 8in (203mm) turrets.

The Myoko class of four heavy cruisers, laid down in 1924–5, were the first Japanese cruisers built to comply with the Washington Treaty limitations. Compared to foreign contemporaries, notably the British County class, they shipped a heavier main armament of 10 8in (203mm) guns and it was claimed that this was made possible by designing the armour protection as an integral part of the ship's structure, thus reducing weight. A refit in the mid-1930s increased the secondary armament to eight 5in (127mm) guns instead of six 4.7in (119mm) and the original fixed torpedo tubes were replaced by four quadruple 24in (610mm) TT. The torpedo and light AA armament was further increased during the war when these four ships formed the 5th Cruiser Division and took part in many actions before being sunk in 1944 or 1945. Notably, *Ashigara* and *Haguro* were sunk by British forces, the latter in a textbook night attack by the 26th Destroyer Flotilla of Penang.

A further four vessels of the Takao class were laid down in 1927–8, and although based on the previous Myoko class, there were several improvements including an increase in both armour protection and the elevation of the main armament to 70 degrees for AA fire (as with the British County class). The Takao class could be distinguished by a massive bridge structure and the fact that the second funnel was upright and not raked. All four ships took part in many major actions and survived until late in the war. Three were sunk during the Leyte Gulf battles of October 1944, while *Takao* managed to escape to Singapore where she was extensively damaged by British midget submarines on 31 July 1945. Although she did not sink, she was captured at the end of the war and scuttled in 1946.

A close-up of the forward section of the heavy cruiser Chokai taken in 1938. The massive bridge and raked fore funnel are clearly shown. (US Navy Historical Branch)

SPECIFICATION

Class: Myoko/Takao (heavy cruiser) Data *Myoko* 1940
Displacement: 10,000 tons (13,300 tons full load)
Length: 631ft (192.3m) pp, 668.5ft (203.8m) oa
Beam: 68ft (20.7m)
Draught: 20ft (6.1m) (mean)
Machinery: 12 boilers, Kanpon geared turbines, 4 shafts, 130,000shp
Speed: 35kt
Range: 8,000nm (14,820km) at 14kt
Complement: 773
Protection: Main belt 4in (102mm), bulkheads 3–4in (76–102mm), decks 1.5in (38mm). Turrets 1in (25mm). Barbettes 3in (76mm). Internal anti-torpedo bulges.
Armament: Guns: 10 8in/203mm (5 × 2), 8 5in/127mm AA (4 × 2), 8 25mm/1in AA (4 × 2), 4 0.5in/13mm AA (2 × 2). Torpedoes: 16 24in (610mm) torpedo tubes (4 × 4).
Aircraft: 3. Two catapults abaft funnels.
Ships in Class: *Myoko, Nachi* (1927); *Haguro, Ashigara* (1928); *Takao, Maya, Atagao* (1930); *Chokai* (1931)

Mogami/Tone

Impression of the heavy cruiser Mogami *at speed showing her armed with 10 8in (203mm) guns.*

Superficially the Mogami class were designed to comply with the limitations laid down by the 1930 London Naval Treaty (10,000 tons maximum displacement and 6in (152mm) calibre guns). In fact, in order to remain within the permitted total tonnage, each individual ship could not exceed 8,500, and this was the nominal tonnage of the completed ships. However, despite every effort to reduce weight, the final design figure was 9,500 tons, and as completed they were even heavier. The overall design was similar to the Takao class, but the two funnels were trunked into a single uptake. The main armament comprised 15 6in guns in five triple turrets with three forward and two aft. The appearance of these heavily armed 'light' cruisers was directly responsible for the subsequent American Brooklyn class and British Southampton class cruisers. In the case of the Japanese ships, the adoption of the 6in gun was a temporary expedient: it was always intended that these ships should be rearmed as soon as possible with 10 8in (203mm) guns, a twin turret replacing each triple 6in. This was done in 1939–40, but prior to that these vessels had proved to be dangerously unstable and were substantially modified and strengthened during refits in 1937–8, adding another 1,000 tons to the standard displacement.

At the start of the war the four Mogami class formed the 7th Cruiser Squadron which took part in the Battle of the Java Sea where *Mogami* and *Mikuma* sank the Allied cruisers USS *Houston* and HMAS *Perth*. Subsequently they were present at Midway where *Mikuma* was sunk by US aircraft. *Mogami* and *Suzuya* were sunk in the Leyte Gulf battles of October 1944, and *Kumano* was sunk off Luzon a month later.

The two Tone class, laid down in 1934–5, were based on the Mogami design but substantially modified in the light of the problems encountered with the earlier ships. They were completed with 8in guns, a total of eight carried in four twin mountings all forward of the bridge, while the after part of the ship was dedicated to the storage and handling of up to eight aircraft. Both ships were lost in the closing stages of the war.

SPECIFICATION

Class: Mogami/Tone (heavy cruiser) Data *Mogami* 1941
Displacement: 12,400 tons (13,887 tons full load)
Length: 620ft (189m) pp, 661ft (201.5m) oa
Beam: 66.25ft (20.2m)
Draught: 19.5ft (5.9m) (mean)
Machinery: 10 boilers (8 in *Suzuya* and *Kumano*), Kanpon geared turbines, 4 shafts, 152,000shp
Speed: 34.5kt
Range: 8,150mm (15,090km) at 14kt
Complement: 850
Protection: Main belt 1–4in (25–102mm), decks 1.25–2.4in (32–61mm). Turrets 1in (25mm). Barbettes 3–4in (76–102mm).
Armament: Guns: 10 8in/203mm (5 × 2), 8 5in/127mm DP (4 × 2), 8 25mm/1in AA (4 × 2), 4 0.5in/13mm AA. Torpedoes: 12 24in (610mm) torpedo tubes (4 × 3).
Aircraft: 3. 2 catapults
Ships in Class: *Mogami, Mikuma, Suzuya* (1934); *Kumano* (1936); *Tone* (1937); *Chikuma* (1938)

Nagara class light cruiser Yura in 1937. The succeeding Sendai class were similar but featured a fourth funnel due to a revised boiler arrangement. (US Navy Historical Branch)

In 1941, Japan had 19 light cruisers whose design was based on World War I experience. The oldest were two 3,200-ton cruisers of the Tenryu class laid down in 1918 and whose design was loosely based on the contemporary British C class. Armed with four 5.5in (140mm) guns and six 21in (533mm) torpedo tubes, they were capable of 33kt and were usually deployed as flagships to destroyer squadrons. These were followed by an enlarged design (Kuma class) of which five were laid down in 1919–20. Displacing 5,000 tons, they carried seven 5.5in guns and eight 21in torpedo tubes, but these latter were replaced by 24in (610mm) tubes in the 1930s. Two of these ships underwent major transformations during the war. In 1941, *Oi* and *Kitikame* had their upper decks widened to accommodate no fewer than 40 24in torpedo tubes in 10 quadruple mountings, five on either beam. *Kitikame* later had the number of torpedo tubes reduced and could also land the others if required so that she could act as a transport and mother ship for up to eight Kaiten midget submarines.

The next group of light cruisers were the six ships of the Nagara class laid down in 1921–3. As completed, they had a fixed flying-off platform over the forward guns in front of the bridge which was itself raised in height so that a seaplane could be stored beneath. In 1934, the aircraft was moved to a catapult more conventionally situated abaft the funnels. One vessel (*Yura*) was lost in 1942, but the remainder were subsequently rearmed with five 5.5in, two 5in (127mm) AA and 24 24in torpedo tubes in six quadruple mountings. However, four were sunk in 1944 and the last (*Isuzu*) was lost in April 1945.

The final embodiment of the 5,000-ton light cruiser was the Sendai class of which three were laid down in 1923–5 (another three were cancelled). They were similar to the Nagara class except that a new boiler arrangement resulted in a fourth funnel, providing an obvious identification feature. Apart from a substantial increase to the light AA armament, they were little modified and all three had been sunk by early 1944.

SPECIFICATION

Class: Sendai (light cruiser) Data *Sendai* 1939
Displacement: 5,110 tons (7,100 tons full load)
Length: 500ft (152.4m) pp, 520ft (158.5m) wl, 535ft (163.1m) oa
Beam: 48.5ft (14.8m)
Draught: 17ft (5.2m) (mean)
Machinery: 12 boilers, Gihon geared turbines, 4 shafts, 90,000shp
Speed: 35.25kt
Range: 7,800nm (14,450km) at 10kt
Complement: 450
Protection: Main belt 2.5in (64mm), decks 2in (51mm).
Armament: Guns: 7 5.5in/140mm (7 × 1), 2 3in/76mm AA (2 × 1), 2 0.5in/13mm AA (2 × 1). Torpedoes: 8 24in (610mm) torpedo tubes (4 × 2). Other: 80 mines.
Aircraft: 1. One catapult aft.
Ships in Class: *Sendai* (1923), *Jintsu* (1923), *Naka* (1925). Also: six Nagara class (1921–3), five Kuma class (1919–20)

DESTROYERS

The destroyer was originally evolved at the end of the nineteenth century in order to protect battlefleets from attacks by small, fast torpedo boats, but subsequently they were also armed with torpedoes and became the prime means of both attack and defence with this weapon. By the outbreak of World War II the destroyer was a true multi-purpose warship, and as well as working with the battlefleet in traditional surface actions it also acted as an anti-submarine escort; many were equipped for minelaying or sweeping, they assisted with defence against air attack, and they supported landing operations. In practice it was found that fleet destroyers were not ideal anti-submarine vessels as their high speed was wasted since the wartime Asdic (or sonar) was not effective at speeds above 20kt. In addition, navies could not afford to have sophisticated destroyers tied up with slow convoys when they were urgently needed for other operations. Consequently, the early war years saw the development of the smaller escort

destroyer which could be rapidly produced in large numbers.

Following the experience of World War I in which there were several fierce destroyer actions, naval strategists between the wars tended to plan for similar encounters in any future conflict. The US Navy laid understandable emphasis on operations in the Pacific Ocean, and many of its destroyers carried a heavy torpedo armament so that long voyages back to a supply base were reduced. The Japanese Navy was faced with the same problem, and uniquely its later destroyers carried additional torpedoes which could be reloaded at sea. Not so obvious was the fact that they had developed the famous Long Lance torpedoes which were much faster and longer-ranged than equivalent Allied weapons, and also carried a much heavier warhead. In the early years of the war this, together with the much superior Japanese skill in night fighting tactics, cost the Allied destroyers dearly. Eventually the US Navy prevailed through a combination of superior numbers, the introduction of radar equipment, and overwhelming air superiority. The first of these factors was a result of the tremendous industrial capacity of the United States, and once this was fully harnessed to war production, standardised designs were produced literally in their hundreds. This was in contrast to Japan, which tended to produce several variations of the various designs, and certainly not on the same scale as the US shipyards.

At the end of World War I, the British Royal Navy was building the V & W class destroyers which were probably the best of the type in the world at the time, and when destroyer production eventually got underway again in the late 1920s an enlarged and more heavily armed version formed the basis for the A to I classes. During the war the similar but slightly larger Emergency Programme destroyers were produced in some numbers. Total British wartime production was 156 destroyers (including escort destroyers) – barely enough to replace the 169 actually lost to various causes. The 1930 London Naval Treaty restricted destroyers to a standard displacement of 1,500 tons but allowed for 'flotilla leaders' of 1,850 tons. As with most treaty rules, this acted as a trigger for navies to build up to the limits specified and gave rise to large destroyers such as the British Tribal and US Porter classes. However, these were also built to counter the trend for larger destroyers already evident among potential enemies such as Germany with their 2,000-ton Maas class and the Japanese Special Type destroyers. Both Italy and France also laid down large destroyers in the 1920s and continued to develop such designs up to 1939.

In general, the larger destroyers did not quite live up to expectations and the standard flotilla vessels tended to perform most tasks just as well. A major factor in World War II was the rapid development of air power, and the Royal Navy in particular suffered grievously in the early war years when it lost dozens of destroyers to air attack, usually while attempting to evacuate the British Army and its Allies from ill-starred campaigns in Norway, France, Greece and Crete. One major factor in this sorry story was that British destroyers did not carry a dual-purpose main armament for use against aircraft, and it was not until the middle of the war that improvements were made in this respect. In fact, it was only in late 1944 that the Battle class with a totally adequate AA armament eventually began to enter service. On the other hand, the US Navy adopted the famous 5in/38cal (127mm) dual-purpose gun well before the war and it was standardised throughout the fleet, providing the secondary armament for battleships, cruisers and aircraft carriers, as well as arming destroyers. The British had a satisfactory twin 4.5in (114mm) DP mounting before the war, but this was only available for battleships and carriers, and a destroyer version took time to develop. Despite this, British destroyers had many successes, notably during the Battle of Narvik in 1940 where the German destroyer flotillas were decimated, and the classic sinking of the Japanese heavy cruiser *Haguro* by the 26th Destroyer Flotilla in 1945.

In the following section all the major British and American destroyer classes are described, together with those of Germany and Japan. Space precludes similar treatment of the French and Italian fleets, but representative classes are included.

Flotilla leader HMS Inglefield. *The 4.7in (119mm) gun in X position has been replaced by a single 4in (102mm) AA.* (Sydney Goodman Collection)

At the end of World War I many older destroyers were scrapped and completion of the later V & W class vessels was slowed down so that for a decade there was no requirement for any new vessels. During the mid-1920s two experimental destroyers, *Amazon* and *Ambuscade*, were built to designs by rival builders Thornycroft and Yarrow. These were in effect a slightly enlarged V & W armed with four 4.7in (119mm) guns and carrying six 21in (533mm) torpedo tubes. As a result of trials with these vessels, a standard Admiralty design was evolved which was slightly larger and carried eight torpedo tubes in two quadruple mountings. With modifications, this basic destroyer type remained in production from 1929 almost up to the outbreak of war 10 years later.

The intention was to build a flotilla of eight vessels, together with one flotilla leader, each year. The flotilla leader was slightly larger than the others to provide additional accommodation and this allowed a fifth 4.7in gun to be mounted between the funnels. The first full flotilla (A class) was laid down in 1929, with the B class following in 1930. The 1931 programme was reduced to four vessels plus a leader and all were transferred to Canada on completion. Nine D class vessels were laid down in 1932 and these introduced the quadruple 0.5in (13mm) machine gun AA mounting for close-range defence. No destroyers were laid down in 1933, but by then the storm clouds of war were beginning to appear and two flotillas (E and F classes) were laid down in 1934. In these, the elevation of the main armament was increased to 40 degrees, but this was too little for effective AA work. The G class was laid down in 1935, and in most of these ships the torpedo armament was increased to 10 (2 × 5). The H class which followed in 1936 was similar but some had a new bridge structure with angled faces which was incorporated into the subsequent I class laid down in 1936–7.

Although not as fast or as heavily armed as some foreign contemporaries, these destroyers gained an excellent reputation and a total of 46 similar destroyers were ordered by foreign navies. At the outbreak of war six vessels were under construction in British yards for Brazil and a further two for Turkey. Similar to the British H class, they were all requisitioned and completed for Royal Navy service. The flotillas described above formed the backbone of the British destroyer force in the early days of the war and a total of 54 were lost to various causes up to 1945. Many were sunk by air attack, painfully highlighting the Achilles' heel of these ships – the lack of a suitable DP gun for their main armament.

SPECIFICATION

Class: A to I classes (destroyer) Data F class as built
Displacement: 1,405 tons (1,940 tons full load)
Length: 318.25ft (97m) pp, 329ft (100.3m) oa
Beam: 33.5ft (10.2m)
Draught: 12.5ft (3.8m) full load
Machinery: 3 boilers, Parsons or Brown-Curtiss SR geared turbines, 2 shafts, 36,000shp
Speed: 35.5kt
Range: 6,350nm (11,760km) at 15kt
Complement: 145
Protection: nil
Armament: Guns: 4 4.7in/119mm (4 × 1), 8 0.5in/13mm AA (2 × 4), 5 .303in (7.7mm) MG (5 × 1). Torpedoes: 8 21in (533mm) torpedo tubes (2 × 4).
Aircraft: nil
Ships in Class: 9 A class (1929), 9 B class (1930), 5 C class (1931), 9 D class (1932), 9 E class (1934), 9 F class (1934), 9 G class (1935), 9 H class (1936), 9 I class (1936–37). All C class transferred to Canada. Finally 8 H/I class initially laid down as export orders for Brazil and Turkey.

HMS Javelin, *as completed, with full torpedo armament. Note X turret trained forward.* (Author's Collection)

The J class, laid down in 1939, was intended as a return to more modest proportions after the Tribal class (cf) and was armed with only six 4.7in (119mm) guns, although an additional bank of torpedo tubes was fitted so that there was little overall loss in offensive capability. The number of boilers was reduced from three to two and the uptakes trunked into a single raked funnel. A flotilla of eight vessels was planned, the custom of building a single larger flotilla leader being abandoned; instead, one of the ships, *Jervis*, had an extended deckhouse aft to allow her to act as leader. The succeeding K class laid down in 1938–9 was similar. War experience again showed the need for a better AA armament and consequently the after bank of torpedo tubes was removed and replaced by a single 4in (102mm) AA gun while the close-range armament was augmented by a number of single 20mm (0.8in) guns. The subsequent production programme moved on to the L and M classes (cf) but in 1940–1 a repeat flotilla of J class was ordered as the N class, though of these eight ships four were transferred to the RAN, two to the Royal Netherlands Navy and one to Poland, so only one actually served with the Royal Navy. They were all completed with a single 4in gun instead of the after torpedo tubes, but this arrangement was reversed from 1942 onwards when the threat of air attack had diminished due to increased availability of carrier-based air support.

No fewer than six J and six K class were lost in the war, all except two in the Mediterranean. One

of these was HMS *Kelly*, commanded by Lord Louis Mountbatten and lost off Crete in May 1941, having previously been badly damaged by a mine in the North Sea in the early months of the war. However, the N class lost only one ship to enemy action (*Nestor*, June 1942).

HMS Nepal *was the only N class destroyer to be Royal Navy-manned during the war. In this view, her after torpedo tubes have been replaced by a 4in (102mm) AA gun.* (Sydney Goodman Collection)

SPECIFICATION

Class: J/K/N classes (destroyer) Data J class as built
Displacement: 1,760 tons (2,330 tons full load)
Length: 339.5ft (103.5m) pp, 356.5ft (108.7m) oa
Beam: 36ft (11m)
Draught: 14ft (4.3m) full load
Machinery: 2 boilers, Parsons SR geared turbines, 2 shafts, 40,000shp
Speed: 36kt
Range: 5,500nm (10,190km) at 15kt
Complement: 183
Protection: nil
Armament: Guns: 6 4.7in/119mm (3 × 2), 4 2pdr AA (1 × 4), 8 0.5in/13mm AA (2 × 4), 4 .303in/7.7mm MG (4 × 1). Torpedoes: 10 21in (533mm) torpedo tubes (2 × 5).
Aircraft: nil
Ships in Class: 8 J class (1938), 8 K class (1938–9), 8 N class (1940–1)

A late war view of HMS Javelin. *She carries a full torpedo armament and a lattice foremast has replaced the original tripod mast.* (Sydney Goodman Collection)

L class destroyer HMS Loyal was completed as designed with six 4.7in (119mm) guns as main armament. (Sydney Goodman Collection)

These two flotillas, each of eight destroyers, were very similar to the J class but with a slightly enlarged hull and increased installed power, although the resulting increase in displacement meant that speed remained the same (c. 32 kt at full load). The main armament remained at six 4.7in (119mm) guns but these were housed in new power-operated enclosed turrets which gave these ships an imposing appearance. Also, the guns could be elevated to 50 degrees giving some improvement in AA capability. When the L class were building, production of the new gun turret did not keep pace and consequently four of the class (*Lance, Larne, Legion, Lively*) were completed with an armament of eight 4in (102mm) AA guns in four twin mountings and also with two banks of quadruple TT. The other four, and all succeeding M class, received the planned main armament, but the after torpedo bank was replaced by a single 4in gun, again to boost the AA defences.

Rushed into action as they were completed, six of the L class were lost in the Mediterranean between 1942 and 1944 while another, *Loyal*, was damaged by mines off the Italian coast in October 1944 to the extent that she was not worth repairing and was subsequently scrapped. Three M class were also sunk, all victims of German U-boats, but four of the survivors were transferred to the Turkish Navy in 1958. Although long since decommissioned, at least one still survives today.

SPECIFICATION

Class: L/M classes (destroyer) Data M class as built
Displacement: 1,920 tons (2,725 tons full load)
Length: 345.5ft (105.3m) pp, 362.25ft (110.4m) oa
Beam: 37ft (11.3m)
Draught: 14.5ft (4.4m) full load
Machinery: 2 boilers, Parsons SR geared turbines, 2 shafts, 48,000shp
Speed: 36kt
Range: 5,500nm (10,190km) at 12kt
Complement: 190
Protection: nil
Armament: Guns: 6 4.7in/119mm DP (3 × 2), 1 4in/102mm AA, 4 2pdr AA (1 × 4), 2 20mm/0.8in AA (2 × 1), 12 0.5in/13mm AA (2 × 4, 2 × 2). Torpedoes: 4 21in (533mm) torpedo tubes (1 × 4).
Aircraft: nil
Ships in Class: Legion (1939); Lance, Larne, Lightning, Lookout (1940); Laforey, Lively, Loyal (1941); Marne, Martin (1940); Milne, Matchless, Meteor, Musketeer (1941); Marksman, Myrmidon (1942)

A pristine-looking HMS Milne*, M class flotilla leader, showing the forward twin 4.7in (119mm) gun turrets to advantage.* (Sydney Goodman Collection)

A stern view of HMS Tartar showing a twin 4in (102mm) AA in X position in lieu of the original 4.7in (119mm) mounting. This modification was extended to most Tribal class destroyers. (Sydney Goodman Collection)

The construction of large destroyers by the German and Japanese navies forced the Admiralty to follow the trend, and after much debate a design featuring eight 4.7in (119mm) guns in four twin mountings and a relatively light torpedo armament of only one quadruple mounting was adopted. Displacement was limited by treaty provisions to 1,850 tons. Known as the Tribal class, no fewer than 16 were laid down in 1937 and the design was also adopted by Australia, which built three, and Canada, which ordered four from British yards and subsequently built four in Canada, although only two of these latter were completed before the end of the war. Almost as soon as hostilities commenced in 1939 it was realised that, despite their imposing appearance, they offered no improvement in AA defence. Consequently X turret was removed and replaced by a twin 4in (102mm) AA mounting controlled by an HA director above the bridge. Surviving vessels later received additional 20mm (0.8in) guns and new radar equipment.

As the navy's most powerful destroyers, they were in the thick of every action; of the first group of seven vessels only one (*Nubian*) survived the war. The second group of nine vessels fared little better, with only three (*Ashanti*, *Eskimo* and *Tartar*) surviving. However, all three Australian vessels saw out the war and only one Canadian vessel (*Athabaskan*) was lost. The latter's name was perpetuated by one of the two Canadian vessels completed after the war to a modified design armed with eight 4in AA guns, a configuration which, with hindsight, might have been better applied to the original design.

SPECIFICATION

Class: Tribal (destroyer) Data *Afridi* as completed 1937
Displacement: 1,960 tons (2,520 tons full load)
Length: 355.5ft (108.4m) pp, 377ft (114.9m) oa
Beam: 36.5ft (11.1m)
Draught: 13ft (4m) full load
Machinery: 2 boilers, Parsons SR geared turbines, 2 shafts, 44,000shp
Speed: 36kt
Range: 5,700nm (10,550km) at 15kt
Complement: 190
Protection: nil
Armament: Guns: 8 4.7in/119mm (4 × 2), 4 2 pdr AA (1 × 4), 8 0.5in/13mm AA (2 × 4). Torpedoes: 4 21in (533mm) torpedo tubes.
Aircraft: nil
Ships in Class: RN: *Afridi*, *Cossack*, *Gurkha*, *Maori*, *Mohawk*, *Nubian*, *Zulu*, *Ashanti*, *Bedouin*, *Eskimo*, *Mashona*, *Matabele*, *Punjabi*, *Sikh*, *Somali*, *Tartar* (1937) RAN: *Arunta* (1940), *Warramunga* (1942), *Bataan* (1944) RCN: *Athabaskan*, *Iroquois* (1941), *Haida*, *Huron* (1942), *Micmac* (1943), *Nootka* (1944), *Cayuga* (1945), *Athabaskan* (ii) (1946)

HMS Nubian *in 1944.* (Maritime Photo Library)

T class destroyer HMS Termagant. *Note the depth-charge racks on the stern, the twin 40mm (1.6in) mounting amidships and a lattice foremast.* (Sydney Goodman Collection)

The cost and complexity of destroyers such as the Tribal and J to N classes led to a simpler 1,500-ton design utilising the machinery of the J class and carrying an armament similar to the earlier H and I classes. Two flotillas were laid down as the O and P classes but the latter were armed with five 4in (102mm) guns (and only one set of quadruple torpedo tubes) to boost the fleet's AA defences. The subsequent Q and R flotillas (each of eight destroyers) reverted to the slightly larger J class hull but were armed with only four single 4.7in (119mm) guns and two sets of quadruple torpedo tubes.

Experience gained with these and earlier destroyers led to the S class, which became the standard British production fleet destroyer for the rest of the war. These were basically similar to the preceding R class with the important difference that the 4.7in guns were carried in a new DP mounting capable of 55 degrees elevation for use against aircraft. A new stabilised 40mm (1.6in) twin mounting was introduced, and up to 12 20mm (0.8in) AA guns were also shipped. The succeeding T, U, V and W flotillas were virtually identical, although some modifications were introduced for each group, the most notable being the adoption of a lattice foremast to carry the increasing amount of radar equipment being fitted. By late 1943 the Z and C classes were also commissioning, and these again were repeats of the basic S class design but introduced a new 4.5in (114mm) DP gun. They were also the last of the standard design to be completed during World War II as the remaining three C class flotillas (Ch, Co, and Cr) were all intended to have remote power control (RPC) for the 4.5in guns together with a new Mk VI HA/LA director, but production difficulties with this equipment delayed their introduction into service.

It is an illustration of how the war was turning in the Allies' favour after 1942 that only five of the Q class and later flotillas (totalling no fewer than 88 destroyers) were lost to enemy action, whereas most of the previous flotillas were decimated in the early war years.

SPECIFICATION

Class: Emergency Programme, O to C flotillas (destroyer) Data S Class as completed 1943
Displacement: 1,710 tons (2,530 tons full load)
Length: 339.5ft (103.5m) pp, 363ft (110.6m) oa
Beam: 35.75ft (10.9m)
Draught: 14ft (4.3m) full load
Machinery: 2 boilers, Parsons SR geared turbines, 2 shafts, 40,000shp
Speed: 36kt
Range: 4,675nm (8,660km) at 20kt
Complement: 170
Protection: nil
Armament: Guns: 4 4.7in/119m DP (4 × 1), 2 40mm/1.6in AA (1 × 2), 8 20mm/0.8in AA (4 × 2). Torpedoes: 8 21in (533mm) torpedo tubes (2 × 4).
Aircraft: nil
Ships in Class: 8 O class (1941–2), 8 P class (1941), 16 Q/R classes (1941–2), 48 S/T/U/V/W/Z classes (1942–4), 32 C class (1943–5)

The P class destroyers were armed with 4in (102mm) guns. HMS Penn *(pennant no. G77) is shown here.* (Author's Collection)

HMS Barfleur *at speed showing wartime camouflage.* (Sydney Goodman Collection)

These were the ultimate British destroyers produced during World War II, although only a few commissioned in time to see active service, mainly with the British Pacific fleet from late 1944 onwards. Design work began in 1941 when it was realised that much greater emphasis on AA capability was required and a twin 4.7in (119mm) DP mounting with 85 degrees elevation was adopted, although the gun was later changed to the 4.5in (114mm) which became the standard destroyer armament. Two twin turrets equipped with RPC were mounted forward and were controlled by a Mk VI HA/LA director, while a substantial battery of 40mm (1.6in), including some in fully stabilised radar controlled mountings, was also fitted. Originally a single 4in (102mm) gun was mounted abaft the funnel and was mainly intended to fire starshell for target illumination. Standard displacement rose to 2,350 tons, making them the largest British destroyers of the war. The hull was similar in length to the Tribal class but beam was substantially increased.

An ambitious construction programme resulted in orders being placed for up to 44 vessels, including four for the RAN. The first group of 16 were all completed, but of 24 vessels in the second group only eight were actually completed (all post-war) and only two RAN vessels were commissioned. The second group were equipped with a US pattern Mk 37 director, shipped a single 4.5in gun abaft the funnel instead of the 4in gun, and torpedo armament was increased from two quadruple to two quintuple mountings.

SPECIFICATION

Class: Battle class (destroyer) Data *Armada* as completed 1944
Displacement: 2,315 tons (3,290 tons full load)
Length: 355ft (108.2m) pp, 379ft (115.5m) oa
Beam: 40.25ft (12.3m)
Draught: 15ft (4.6m) full load
Machinery: 2 boilers, Parsons SR geared turbines, 2 shafts, 50,000shp
Speed: 34kt
Range: 4,400nm (8,150km) at 20kt
Complement: 247/308
Protection: nil
Armament: Guns: 4 4.5in/114mm DP (2 × 2), 1 4in/102mm DP, twelve 40mm/1.6in AA (4 × 2, 4 × 1). Torpedoes: 8 21in (533mm) torpedo tubes (2 × 4).
Aircraft: nil
Ships in Class: First Group: *Armada, Barfleur* (1943); *Cadiz, Camperdown, Finisterre, Gravelines, Hogue, Lagos, St Kitts, Saintes, Solebay, Trafalgar* (1944); *Gabbard, St James, Sluys, Vigo* (1945). Second Group: 11 vessels (1945–6) RAN: 2 vessels (1947–8)

HMS Solebay *leaving the River Tyne after completion in 1944. Note the concentration of 40mm (1.6in) guns aft.* (Sydney Goodman Collection)

HMS Wishart, *a Modified W class destroyer, photographed in 1937.* (Author's Collection)

By the end of World War I in 1918 the V & W class destroyers were probably the best of their type in service anywhere at that time. A total of 59 were eventually commissioned, and by the mid-1930s some 52 remained available for service, others having been scrapped to allow for new construction under the terms of the various naval treaties. The original V & W classes were armed with four 4in (102mm) guns, and the later Modified W class with four 4.7in (119mm) guns, while most eventually standardised on a torpedo armament of two sets of triple 21in (533mm) tubes.

In 1938, work began to convert the 4in armed V & W classes to fast escort vessels, but this programme was thrown into disarray by the outbreak of war and subsequently a number of different modification programmes were implemented, some vessels undergoing more than one conversion. At least 10 vessels, including those manned by the RAN, underwent little change apart from an increase in light AA armament and continued to be employed as conventional destroyers. As originally envisaged, the fast escort conversion involved the replacement of the original main armament with two twin 4in AA, the removal of the torpedo tubes and the addition of depth-charge mortars and stern racks. As the war progressed, most were fitted with radar and MF/DF. For convoy escort duties radius of action was more useful than speed, and a number of vessels were converted to long-range escorts by the removal of the forward boiler and funnel which gave additional bunker capacity as well as extra accommodation and stowage space.

They generally retained three 4in or 4.7in guns, although eventually the forward gun was replaced by a Hedgehog ATW. Other V & W class had a reduced main armament so that additional A/S weapons could be fitted, but retained their original machinery so that they were known as short-range escorts.

Despite their age, the V & W class destroyers gave sterling service during the war and 19 were lost in action.

SPECIFICATION

Class: V & W (destroyer) Data V/W class 1939
Displacement: 1,100 tons (1,460 tons full load)
Length: 300ft (91.4m) pp, 312ft (95.1m) oa
Beam: 29.5ft (9m)
Draught: 11.75ft (3.6m) full load
Machinery: 3 boilers, Parsons or Brown-Curtiss SR geared turbines, 2 shafts, 27,000shp
Speed: 34kt
Range: 3,500nm (6,480km) at 15kt
Complement: 134
Protection: nil
Armament: Guns: 4 4in/102mm (4 × 1), 1 2pdr AA, 5 MG. Torpedoes: 6 21in (533mm) torpedo tubes (2 × 3).
Aircraft: nil
Ships in Class: Available in 1939: 23 V class (1917–18), 19 W class (1917–18), 15 modified W class (1918–19)

Wickes/Clemson

HMS Churchill *was a Wickes/Clemson class destroyer transferred to the Royal Navy in 1940.* (Author's Collection)

When America entered World War I in 1917 the US Navy had a relatively small destroyer fleet but immediately placed orders for hundreds of the four-stack flush-decked Wickes and Clemson class. Very few of these were completed in time to see service before the 1918 armistice, but production continued until 1922 when no fewer than 273 had been completed. During the inter-war years, the numbers available were reduced, noticeably by the 1930 London Naval Treaty which resulted in 93 being scrapped, some of which had been laid up on completion and had seen no active service.

In 1940, 50 were transferred to the Royal Navy and most were converted into anti-submarine escorts to provide sorely needed relief to the North Atlantic convoys. At the time of Pearl Harbor, a total of 71 were available to the US Navy for use as destroyers, although several others had been converted for other tasks such as fast troop transports, fast minelayers or minesweepers. This process continued during World War II, but many were also converted to anti-submarine escorts along the lines of the RN vessels. Modifications included removal of the after boiler and funnel which allowed extra fuel oil to be carried, topweight was reduced by shortening masts and funnels (as completed, these boats were notoriously uncomfortable in rough weather), and they were rearmed with six 3in (76mm) guns. The after torpedo tubes were removed and depth charge racks and stowage

were fitted right aft. At a later stage some vessels received a Hedgehog ATW on the forecastle.

The vessels transferred to the Royal Navy were all renamed after towns whose name were common to both Britain and the United States. One of these, *Campbeltown*, was altered to resemble a German torpedo boat and, packed with explosives, was expended in the famous raid on the St Nazaire drydock in March 1942.

SPECIFICATION

Class: Wickes/Clemson (destroyer) Data Clemson class pre-1941
Displacement: 1,190 tons (1,590 tons full load)
Length: 310ft (94.5m) wl, 314.5ft (95.9m) oa
Beam: 31.75ft (9.7m)
Draught: 9ft (2.7m) standard
Machinery: 4 boilers, geared turbines, 3 shafts, 26,000shp
Speed: 35kt
Range: 5,000nm (9,260km) at 14kt
Complement: 153
Protection: nil
Armament: Guns: 4 4in/102mm (4 × 1), 1 3in/76mm AA, 2 0.5in/13mm AA (2 × 1). Torpedoes: 12 21in (533mm) torpedo tubes (4 × 3).
Aircraft: nil
Ships in Class: 71 in service in December 1941

Farragut class destroyer USS **MacDonough** *(DD 351). (Wright & Logan Collection)*

With hundreds of the older flush-decked destroyers available, the US Navy was in no hurry to recommence destroyer construction and it was not until 1932 that the first of eight Farragut class were laid down. They were very similar in size and layout to contemporary British destroyers but with the major difference of having a fully dual-purpose main armament in the form of 5in/38cal (127mm) guns with an associated combined HA/LA director. The succeeding Mahan class were basically similar but the torpedo armament was increased to 12 torpedo tubes by replacing the single after quadruple mount by two quadruple mounts, one on either beam. The funnels were more widely spaced and of equal width, whereas the Farragut class had the two funnels set close together with the after one broader than the fore funnel. In both classes the forward gun mountings were protected by weatherproof gunshields, but the after guns were on open mountings. Two of the last Mahan class were completed with the forward guns in fully enclosed gunhouses, which became standard on most subsequent construction.

Cassin and *Downes* were caught in drydock at Pearl Harbor and were damaged beyond repair, although their armament, machinery and other equipment were salvaged and installed in newly constructed hulls of the same name so that, officially, they were never lost. *Hull* and *Monaghan* were lost in unusual circumstances when they foundered with very heavy loss of life during a typhoon off Luzon on 18 December 1944. Other war losses included *Worden*, *Mahan*, and *Reid*.

SPECIFICATION:

Class: Farragut/Mahan (destroyer) Data *Farragut* as built
Displacement: 1,365 tons (2,230 tons full load)
Length: 330ft (100.6m) wl, 341.5ft (104.1m) oa
Beam: 34.5ft (10.5m)
Draught: 16ft (3.2m) full load
Machinery: 4 boilers, Parsons SR geared turbines, 2 shafts, 42,800shp
Speed: 36.5kt
Range: n/a
Complement: 250
Protection: nil
Armament: Guns: 5 5in/127mm DP (5 × 1), 4 0.30in/7.6mm AA (4 × 1). Torpedoes: 8 21in (533mm) torpedo tubes (2 × 4).
Aircraft: nil
Ships in Class: *Farragut, Dewey, Hull, MacDonough, Worden, Aylwin* (1934); *Dale, Monaghan* (1935); *Mahan, Cummings, Flusser, Case, Conyngham, Cassin, Shaw, Cushing, Perkins* (1935); *Drayton, Lamson, Reid, Tecker, Downes, Smith, Preston* (1936); *Dunlap, Fanning* (1936)

USS Somers (DD 381) in 1938. Similar in size to the British Tribal class, they carried a much heavier torpedo armament.
(Wright & Logan Collection)

The Porter class of eight large destroyers were contemporary to the British Tribal class and were very similar in size although more heavily armed. The gun armament of eight 5in (127mm) DP in four twin mountings was much the same but a heavier torpedo armament was shipped and there were two multiple 1.1in (28mm) AA mountings. This, together with other features, made them rather top heavy and during World War II additional close-range armament could only be fitted at the expense of other fittings and equipment. By 1945 most carried only four or five 5in guns, the after director was removed, funnels shortened and the bridge reduced in height. This allowed around eight 20mm (0.8in) and three twin 40mm (1.6in) mountings to be added. Only the name ship, USS *Porter* (DD 356), was lost during the war, torpedoed by a Japanese submarine off Santa Cruz on 26 October 1942.

A further five similar destroyers were completed in 1938–9 to modified design intended to reduced topweight. These consisted of two Somers class and three Sampson class. All featured a reduced superstructure and the boiler uptakes were trunked into a single funnel. Armament was similar except that an extra bank of torpedo tubes was fitted in the space resulting from the changed funnel arrangements, making a total of three quadruple mounts in the case of the Somers class and three triple in the case of the Sampson

class. None was lost to enemy action, but the USS *Warrington* foundered off the Bahamas during a storm in September 1944. War modifications were similar to those of the Porter class.

SPECIFICATION

Class: Porter/Somers (destroyer) Data Porter class as built
Displacement: 1,850 tons (2,840 tons full load)
Length: 371ft (113.1m) wl, 381ft (116.1m) oa
Beam: 37ft (11.3m)
Draught: 17ft (5.2m) full load
Machinery: 4 boilers, Parsons SR geared turbines, 2 shafts, 50,000shp

Speed: 37kt
Range: n/a
Complement: Up to 290
Protection: nil
Armament: Guns: 8 5in/127mm SP (4 × 2), 8 1.1in/128mm AA (2 × 4), 2 0.5in/13mm AA (2 × 1). Torpedoes: 8 21in (533mm) torpedo tubes (2 × 4).

Aircraft: nil
Ships in Class: *Porter, Phelps, Clark, Moffet* (1935); *Selfridge, McDougal, Winslow, Balch* (1936); *Somers, Warrington, Sampson* (1937); *Davis, Jouett* (1938)

Gridley/Benham/Sims

Gridley class destroyer USS Blue *(DD 387), as completed. Note the after 5in (127mm) guns in open mountings.* (US Navy Historical Branch)

Despite the increasing power of naval aviation, US naval strategists in the inter-war years still envisaged Jutland-type battles between conventional surface fleets each employing numerous destroyer flotillas. A heavy torpedo armament was therefore deemed necessary to counter the similarly armed Japanese destroyers, and the Gridley/Benham classes carried no fewer than 16 21in (533mm) torpedo tubes in four quadruple mountings arranged in two banks on either beam. Despite this increase in armament, these ships basically utilised the same hull as the earlier Mahan class, although the boiler uptakes were trunked into a single funnel. A total of 10 Gridley and 12 Benham class were completed by 1938, the main difference between them being that the former had four boilers while the latter had only three. In common with earlier American destroyers, only the fore turrets were fully enclosed, the after 5in (127mm) guns being in open mountings.

The 12 Sims class completed in 1939–40 were similar but the torpedo armament was reduced to two quadruple mounts, both on the centreline, while hull dimensions were slightly increased to an overall length of 348ft (106.1m). War modifications to all three classes generally consisted of additional light AA guns while most of the Gridley and Benham classes had the two after torpedo mountings removed. War losses included *Blue, Henley, Jarvis, Benham, Rowan, Sims, Hamman, O'Brien, Walke* and *Morris*. Most of these losses were incurred in the fierce battles around Guadalcanal in 1942, but *Rowan* was torpedoed by a German E-boat off Salerno in the Mediterranean in September 1943.

SPECIFICATION

Class: Gridley/Benham/Sims (destroyer) Data Gridley class as built
Displacement: 1,500 tons (2,350 tons full load)
Length: 334ft (101.8m) wl, 341ft (103.9m) oa
Beam: 35.5ft (10.8m)
Draught: 17ft (5.2m) full load
Machinery: 4 boilers, geared turbines, 2 shafts, 50,000shp
Speed: 38kt
Range: 6,000nm (11,110km) at 15kt
Complement: 250+
Protection: nil
Armament: Guns: 4 5in/127mm DP (4 × 1), 4 0.5in/13mm AA (4 × 1). Torpedoes: 16 21in (533mm) torpedo tubes (4 × 4).
Aircraft: nil
Ships in Class: *Gridley, Bagley, Mugford, Ralph Talbot* (1936); *Craven, Blue, Helm, Henley, Patterson, Jarvis* (1937); *McCall* (1937); *Benham, Ellet, Lang, Maury, Mayrant, Trippe, Rhind, Rowan, Stack, Sterrett* (1938); *Wilson* (1939); *Sims, Mustin, Russell* (1938), *Hughes, Anderson, Hamman, O'Brien, Walke, Morris, Roe, Wainright, Buck* (1939)

USS Mustin *(DD 413), a Sims class destroyer, shown wearing camouflage in June 1942. After 5in (127mm) gun is in an enclosed mounting.* (US Navy Historical Branch)

Benson class destroyer USS Lansdale *(DD 426) was lost while escorting an Atlantic convoy on 20 April 1944.* (Author's Collection)

With the Benson/Livermore class the US Navy built on experience already gained to produce a standard fleet destroyer suitable for mass production, and the true capacity of the US shipbuilding industry becomes apparent when reviewing the numbers built over a four-year period, although this was eclipsed by the staggering production rates achieved with subsequent vessels. The hull was similar to the Sims class but a unit machinery system of alternate boiler and engine rooms was adopted so that two well-spaced funnels were required. By adopting quintuple mountings a heavy torpedo armament could be shipped on the centreline, although this was carried atop the extended machinery casing superstructure which was a feature of all American destroyer designs. The only visual difference between the two classes was that the Benson class had flat-sided funnels while the Livermore class had rounded funnels. Four vessels (*Lansdale*, *Gwin*, *Meredith* and *Monssen*) were war losses.

The succeeding Bristol class were basically repeats of the earlier class except that they were completed with only four 5in (127mm) guns, although these were all in fully enclosed turrets, and the light AA armament was enhanced as a result of early war experience in Europe. Later, most were modified by the removal of one bank of torpedo tubes and the light AA armament increased eventually to four 40mm (1.6in) and six or seven 20mm (0.8in) guns. Towards the end of the Pacific war, 24 Bristol class were modified as fast minesweepers (DMS) with Y turret removed to make room for the sweeping gear on the fantail. A total of 15 Bristol class were lost during the war.

SPECIFICATION

Class: Benson/Livermore/Bristol (destroyer) Data *Benson* 1940
Displacement: 1,620 tons (2,515 tons full load)
Length: 341ft (103.9mm) wl, 348ft (106.1m) oa
Beam: 35.5ft (10.8m)
Draught: 17.5ft (5.3m) full load
Machinery: 4 boilers, geared turbines, 2 shafts, 50,000shp
Speed: 37.5kt
Range: 6,000nm (11,110km) at 15kt
Complement: 276
Protection: nil
Armament: Guns: 5 5in/127mm DP (5 × 1), 6 0.5in/13mm AA (6 × 1). Torpedoes: 10 21in (533mm) torpedo tubes (2 × 5).
Aircraft: nil
Ships in Class: Benson class: 32 ships (1939–42)
Livermore class: 64 ships (1940–3)
Bristol class: 73 ships (1941–3)

USS Woodworth *(DD 460), Bristol class destroyer completed in 1942.* (Maritime Photo Library)

USS Isherwood (DD 520), a Fletcher class destroyer launched in October 1942. (Sydney Goodman Collection)

The Fletcher class represented the ultimate refinement of the basic pre-war US fleet destroyer and the staggering total of 175 vessels of this type were all completed during World War II. With the US entry into the war in December 1941, orders were initially boosted to 124, although 11 of this first group were cancelled in favour of other orders. The Fletcher class were slightly larger than their predecessors and standard displacement rose to just over 2,000 tons. The hull was flush-decked with a marked sheer forward. The increased dimensions enabled a substantial light AA armament to be fitted while still retaining the full gun and torpedo armament. The first examples carried four 1.1in (28mm) and six 20mm (0.8in) AA guns, but this was gradually increased in subsequent vessels until the last to be completed were armed with 10 40mm (1.6in) and seven 20mm AA guns. Interestingly, six vessels were intended to carry an aircraft on a trainable catapult abaft the after fun-

nel, but only three (*Pringle, Stevens* and *Halford*) were so fitted. The experiment was not a success, a destroyer proving too small to satisfactorily operate the aircraft, and the equipment was subsequently removed. Follow-on orders were placed for a second group of 62 Fletcher class, these differing mainly in that the HA/LA director was not so high up above the bridge, and almost all were completed with the full outfit of 40mm and 20mm guns. Many Fletcher class were named after destroyers that had been lost in the early actions of the war, and one famous example, USS *The Sullivans* (DD 537), commemorated a whole family of five brothers lost aboard the cruiser USS *Juneau* in November 1942.

USS Kidd (DD 661), a Fletcher class destroyer commissioned in mid-1943. (Author's Collection)

SPECIFICATION

Class: Fletcher (destroyer) Data USS *Dyson* 1944
Displacement: 2,050 tons (2,940 tons full load)
Length: 369.25ft (112.5m) wl, 376.5ft (114.8m) oa
Beam: 39.5ft (12m)
Draught: 17.75ft (5.4m) full load
Machinery: 4 boilers, geared turbines, 2 shafts, 60,000shp
Speed: 37kt
Range: 6,000nm (11,110km) at 15kt
Complement: c. 330
Protection: nil
Armament: Guns: 5 5in/127mm DP (5 × 1), 6 40mm/1.6in AA (3 × 2), 10 20mm/0.8in AA (10 × 1). Torpedoes: 10 21in (533mm) torpedo tubes (2 × 5).
Aircraft: 1. One catapult – in 3 ships only.
Ships in Class: 175 ships (1942–4)

UNITED STATES
Sumner/Gearing

USS Samuel B. Roberts *(DD 823) was one of several Gearing class destroyers completed just after the war.* (Author's Collection)

The Sumner class was based on the highly successful Fletcher class but beam was slightly increased so that three twin 5in/38cal (127mm) twin mountings could be shipped as main armament while a heavy battery of 40mm (1.6in) and 20mm (0.8in) guns was also fitted, giving these ships the substantial AA capability which was shown to be essential durinng the Pacific war. A full torpedo armament of 10 21in (533mm) tubes was also shipped, making these some of the most heavily armed destroyers built during the war. Twelve Sumner class were modified to act as fast minelayers (DM), and in these the upper deck aft was cleared to provide room to stow up to 100 mines, this necessitating the removal of the after bank of torpedo tubes and some 20mm guns as compensation. Many of the class were in the forefront of the operations to occupy Okinawa in 1945, and four were lost to air and kamikaze attacks while many more were seriously damaged.

The Gearing class were essentially repeats of the Sumner class except that the hull was lengthened

amidships by 14ft (4.3m) to provide additional accommodation and stowage space, standard displacement creeping up to almost 2,500 tons. Once again, a substantial light AA armament was shipped, and with the appearance of the kamikaze threat some had their after torpedo tubes replaced by a quadruple 40mm mounting. By the closing stages of the war it was recognised that even the 40mm gun could not cope with kamikaze attacks where even mortally wounded aircraft ploughed into their target, and some Gearing class began to receive a rapid-firing 3in/50cal (76mm) gun instead. Although this weapon was widely adopted after the war, few ships had been fitted before the end of hostilities. Some 22 Gearing class were modified to act as radar pickets (DDR), and in these the forward torpedo tubes were replaced by a lattice mast carrying a long-range air warning radar. Deployed forward of the fleet to give early warning of air attacks, these DDR were prime kamikaze targets and suffered heavily while performing this vital task, although none was actually lost.

A post-war view of the Sumner class destroyer USS Douglas H. Fox *(DD 779) at Malta in 1947.* (Wright & Logan Collection)

USS Bordelon *(DD 881) was one of several Gearing class destroyers completed as radar pickets, distinguishable by the tripod mainmast between the funnels.* (Wright & Logan Collection)

SPECIFICATION

Class: Sumner/Gearing (destroyer) Data Sumner class
Displacement: 2,200 tons (3,515 tons full load)
Length: 369ft (112.5m) wl, 376ft (114.6m) oa
Beam: 41ft (12.5m)
Draught: 19ft (5.8m) full load
Machinery: 4 boilers, geared turbines, 2 shafts, 60,000shp
Speed: 34kt
Range: 6,000nm (11,110km) at 15kt
Complement: 336–363
Protection: nil
Armament: Guns: 6 5in/127mm DP (3 x 2), 12 40mm/1.6in AA (2 X 4, 2 x 2), 11 20mm/0.8in AA (11 x 1). Torpedoes: 10 21in (533mm) torpedo tubes (2 x 5), except in ships fitted for minelaying. Other: 100 mines in 12 ships.
Aircraft: nil
Ships in Class: Sumner class: 58 ships (1943–4) Gearing class: 105 ships (1944–7) – includes 6 cancelled before completion and 4 completed in 1949 to a post-war modified design. Orders for 51 other vessels were cancelled in 1945.

91

Buckley/Rudderow

USS Reybold *(DE 177) was transferred to Brazil on completion in 1944. Renamed* Bauru, *it is preserved today in Rio de Janeiro.* (Author's Collection)

The destroyer escort construction programme was one of the largest industrial undertakings of the war, and at one point over 1,000 had been ordered although in the event only 563 were actually completed, itself a fantastic achievement. Production started in 1942 and peaked in the last three months of 1943 when no fewer than 125 were launched.

The origins of the destroyer escort (DE) lay in an urgent British requirement for ocean escorts. With shipyards at home fully stretched, an order for 50 escorts was placed with American yards under the newly introduced Lend Lease scheme. The specification called for a length of around 300ft (91m), a speed of 20kt and a good endurance. The design was left to the Americans who, in effect, produced a miniature flush-decked destroyer which eventually was built in several variants. The first was the diesel electric-powered Evarts class (known as the Captain class in the Royal Navy) of which 97 were built. These were followed by no fewer than 152 Buckley class in which steam turbo electric machinery was adopted to boost speed to 24kt although this necessitated a slight increase in hull length. Many DEs were rearmed with two single 5in (127mm) guns instead of the three 3in (76mm) guns originally fitted, and the Rudderow class (81 vessels) was basically a repeat of the Buckleys but with the 5in guns as standard. In the meantime, bottlenecks in the supply of the steam plants led to reversion to diesel electric propulsion in the Canon class (76 built), although the longer hull was retained. The Edsall class, of which 85 were built, was diesel-powered with reduction gears instead of the electric drive, while the ultimate John C.

Butler class (74 vessels) were similar to the Rudderow except that the steam turbines were directly connected to the shafts through reduction gears and the electric drive was also abandoned. With a short funnel, solid bridge structure and 5in guns, the profile of these last DEs differed substantially from the original ships. Of the total built, 56 were completed as fast transports (ADP), 78 were transferred to the Royal Navy, and 12 to France and Brazil.

SPECIFICATION

Class: Buckley/Rudderow (destroyer escort) Data Buckley class
Displacement: 1,400 tons (1,720 tons full load)
Length: 300ft (91.4m) wl, 306ft (93.3m) oa
Beam: 37ft (11.3m)
Draught: 13.5ft (4.1m) full load
Machinery: 2 boilers, General Electric turbines and electric motors, 2 shafts, 12,000shp
Speed: 24kt
Range: 5,500nm (10,190km) at 15kt
Complement: 220
Protection: nil
Armament: Guns: 3 3in/76mm DP (3 × 1), 4 1.1in/28mm AA (1 × 4), 8 20mm/0.8in AA (8 × 1). Torpedoes: 3 21in (533mm) torpedo tubes (1 × 3). Other: Hedgehog A/S mortar, DCTs.
Aircraft: nil
Ships in Class: Buckley class: 152 completed (1942–4) Rudderow class: 81 completed (1943–5) Also 97 Evarts, 85 Edsall, 76 Canon and 74 John C. Butler classes.

The French super destroyer Le Triomphant. *(Sydney Goodman Collection)*

The French Navy could reasonably lay claim to having started the cycle in which several navies felt compelled to build large, heavily armed destroyers to supplement the standard flotillas. In 1917 design studies began on a super destroyer capable of 35kt and armed with 5.5in (140mm) guns. Subsequent experience with the captured German 2,500-ton *S113* was also incorporated in the six Jaguar class ordered in 1922 and commissioned in 1925. These were armed with five 5in (127mm) guns in single mounts and six 21.7in (550mm) torpedo tubes. Displacing some 2,400 tons, they easily made 35kt and were visually identifiable by their three funnels. Improvements in the design led to the slightly larger Guepard class, of which 18 were launched between 1928 and 1931. Variations introduced resulted in four separate sub-groups, but all were armed with five 5.5in guns, although later ships had the Mk 1927 semi-automatic weapon with a much increased rate of fire. Torpedo armament was increased from six to seven tubes (1 × 3 and 2 × 2) and some were fitted for minelaying, carrying up to 50 1,100lb (500kg) mines. Once again, these were very fast ships, capable of over 36kt at full load and achieving over 42kt in trial conditions. They were also unique among ships of the period in having four funnels.

The ultimate development of this type of destroyer was the Le Fantasque class laid down in 1931 and completed in 1935–6. These were essentially similar to the Guepard class except that the uptakes from the four boilers were trunked into two widely spaced funnels giving these ships a much more modern appearance. There was no mainmast and a number of aerials were therefore attached to the after funnel. Like many French warships in World War II, the six Le Fantasque class had chequered wartime careers. Initially they worked in conjunction with British forces, but in 1940 *Le Triomphant* joined the Free French Navy. Others were involved in actions against Allied forces at Oran and Dakar. Following the German occupation of Vichy France in 1942, *L'Indomptable* was scuttled at Toulon and *L'Audacieux* was sunk by Allied aircraft in 1943. The remaining three eventually joined the Allied cause and were refitted in the United States before returning for service in the Mediterranean until the end of the war.

A stern view of Le Triomphant **showing the after 5.5in (140mm) guns.**

SPECIFICATION

Class: Le Fantasque (destroyer) Data as completed
Displacement: 2,569 tons (3,400 tons full load)
Length: 411ft (125.3m) pp, 434ft (132.3m) oa
Beam: 40.5ft (12.3m)
Draught: 16.5ft (5m)
Machinery: 4 small tube boilers, 2 shafts, Parsons or Rateau-Bretagne SR geared turbines, 74,000shp
Speed: 37kt
Range: 4,000nm (7,412km) at 15kt
Complement: 210
Protection: nil
Armament: Guns: 5 5.5in/140mm (5 × 1), 4 37mm/1.45in AA (4 × 1). Torpedoes: 9 21.7in (550mm) torpedo tubes (3 × 3). Other: racks for 16 depth charges, up to 50 1,100lb (500kg) mines.
Aircraft: nil
Ships in Class: Le Fantasque, L'Audacieux, Le Malin, Le Terrible, Le Triomphant (1931); L'Indomptable (1932)

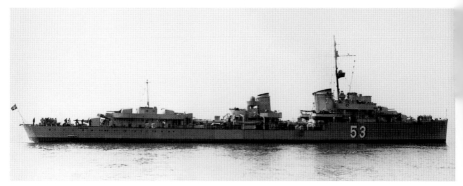

Von Roeder class destroyer **Hans Lüdemann** *(Z18).* (WZ Bilddienst)

The **Bruno Heinemann** *(Z8) was one of sixteen Maas class destroyers.* (WZ Bilddienst)

1935 was a watershed year for the German Navy as Hitler openly declared that Germany no longer accepted the restrictions of the Versailles Treaty which, in the case of flotilla vessels, had limited construction to torpedo boats of 600 tons or less. In order to support the new capital ships then ordered or under construction, much larger fleet destroyers would be needed, and the first group of 16 were laid down in 1935–7. Known as the Leberecht Maas class and allocated pennant numbers Z1 to Z16 (Z denoting *Zerstörer*), they were considerably larger than many foreign destroyers although the armament of five 5in (127mm) guns and eight 21in (533mm) torpedo tubes was relatively conservative. They were handsome ships but their weak point, as with many other German warships of the period, was the high-pressure boiler system which was prone to breakdowns and susceptible to battle damage. Another six similar destroyers of the Von Roeder class (Z17–Z22) were laid down in 1937–8.

Both classes were extensively deployed during the 1940 Norwegian campaign, and no fewer than 10 were sunk or scuttled during the Narvik fjord battles. Another two (Z1 and Z3) had previously been sunk in error by German aircraft in the North Sea in February 1940. The surviving vessels were generally modified by the removal of C turret and the addition of extra 37mm (1.45in) and 20mm (0.8in) AA guns. Of those vessels which survived in 1945, four were ceded to the Royal Navy, and two of these transferred to the French Navy in 1946. Another three were transferred to Russia.

SPECIFICATION

Class: Maas/Von Roeder (destroyer) Data Z1–Z4 as completed
Displacement: 2,250 tons (3,150 tons full load)
Length: 374ft (114m) pp, 390ft (118.9m) oa
Beam: 37ft (11.3m)
Draught: 14ft (4.3m) full load
Machinery: 6 very high-pressure boilers, 2 shafts, geared turbines, 70,000shp
Speed: 38kt
Range: 4,400nm (8,150km) at 19kt
Complement: 315
Protection: nil
Armament: Guns: 5 5in/127mm (5 × 1), 4 37mm/1.45in AA (2 × 2). Torpedoes: 8 21in (533mm) tubes (2 × 4). Other: 60 mines.
Aircraft: nil
Ships in Class: Leberecht Maas (Z1–Z16): 5 (1935), 8 (1936), 3 (1937). Von Roeder (Z17–Z22): 1 (1938), 5 (1939).

Narvik class destroyer Z27 photographed in a Norwegian fjord. (WZ Bilddienst)

The Z23 and subsequent classes of German destroyers, sometimes referred to as the Narvik class, sought to further offset numerical deficiency by increasing the fighting power of individual destroyers. Based on the preceding Von Roeder class, the main armament was increased to 5.9in (150mm) guns carried in one twin mounting forward and three single mountings aft, although almost all were initially completed with only a single 5.9in gun forward until the twin mounting became available in 1942. However, by that time C gun aft was being removed so that the light AA armament could be supplemented, and by 1945 Z25, for example, carried 10 37mm (1.45in) and 16 20mm (0.8in) AA guns. Given the slower rate of fire of the 5.9in gun, and the difficulty of accurate fire control aboard relatively small and lively ships, the adoption of the larger gun really had little practical advantage, a fact tacitly admitted by the construction of five destroyers (Z35, 36, 43–45) later in the war in which the main armament reverted to five 5in (127mm) guns in single mountings.

The Narvik class was built in two sub-groups of which the first (Z23–30) were launched in 1939–40, and only three survived to 1945 when Britain, America and France each received one example. Although the first two were scrapped after various trials, the French Navy kept theirs in service (renamed *Hoche*) for several years. The next group of seven ships were completed later in the war and only two were lost during hostilities, the survivors being shared out among the Allies.

SPECIFICATION

Class: Z23 (Narvik) (destroyer) Data Z23 as built
Displacement: 2,600 tons (3,600 tons full load)
Length: 393ft (119.8m) pp, 416ft (126.8m) oa
Beam: 39ft (11.9m)
Draught: 15ft (4.6m) full load
Machinery: 6 very high-pressure boilers, Wagner geared turbines, 2 shafts, 70,000shp
Speed: 38kt
Range: 5,000nm (9,260km) at 19kt
Complement: 321
Protection: nil
Armament: Guns: 5 5.9in/150mm (1 × 2 and 3 × 1),
6 37mm/1.45in AA (2 × 2 and 2 × 1).
Torpedoes: 8 21in (533mm) tubes (2 × 4).
Other: 60 mines.
Aircraft: nil
Ships in Class: Z23 (1939), Z24–Z30 (1940), Z31–Z33 and Z37–Z39 (1941), Z34 (1942) – 15 in total.

Nicolo Zeno*, the last of twelve Navigatori class destroyers to be built, was completed in 1930.* (WZ Bilddienst)

The Navigatori class of destroyers were built in response to the French Jaguar and Guepard class super destroyers, although at just over 2,000 tons they were not quite as large. Most of the previous Italian destroyers built after World War I were much smaller, the preceding Sauro and Turbine classes displacing around 1,000 tons (standard). The Navigatori class, named after famous navigators and seamen, were loosely based on the three Leone class scouts laid down in 1921, and as completed were armed with six 4.7in (119mm) guns in three twin mountings unusually arranged with one fore and aft and the other amidships between the funnels. On initial trials in very artificial conditions one of these destroyers recorded a speed of 44kt, but a typical maximum under light load was 38kt. In 1939–40 all but two of the class were modified by the addition of a flared and raked bow and a widening of the hull to improve stability with the result that maximum speed at full load dropped to around 30kt.

After the Navigatori class, Italian destroyer construction reverted to more modest vessels although size gradually crept up from the 1,200 tons of the Dardo and Folgore classes (laid down 1929–30) to the 1,600-tons of the Maestrale and Oriani classes (1931–36). The Soldati class continued this trend and followed the same layout with a raised forecastle carried aft to abreast a single broad raked funnel. The first were laid down in 1937 and a total of 19 units in two groups were laid down, although two were never completed. The main difference between the two groups was in the main armament which in the first group generally consisted of four 4.7in/50cal (119mm) guns in twin mountings fore and aft, and a single 4.7in/15cal lighting howitzer amidships. However, in the second group most had an additional 4.7in/50cal instead of the lighting howitzer. Both groups were fitted for minelaying and could stow up to 48 mines. During the course of the war, one set of torpedo tubes was removed from some vessels and replaced by a twin 37mm (1.45in) AA mounting.

Destroyer Lanciere *running trials in 1939.* (Robert Hunt Library)

SPECIFICATION		
Class: Navigatori (destroyer) Data after reconstruction 1939–40		
Displacement: 2,125 tons (2,888 tons full load)		
Length: 351ft (107m) pp, 353.5ft (107.7m) oa		
Beam: 36.75ft (11.2m)		
Draught: 12ft (3.7m)		
Machinery: 4 boilers, geared turbines, 2 shafts, 55,000shp		
Speed: c. 30kt		
Range: 3,800nm (7,040km) at 18kt		
Complement: 225		
Protection: nil		
Armament: Guns: 6 4.7in/119mm (3 × 2), 7 or 9 20mm/0.8in AA (7/9 × 1). Torpedoes: 6 21in (533mm) in torpedo tubes (2 × 3). Other: up to 104 mines.		
Aircraft: nil		
Ships in Class: *Giovanni da Verrazzano, Luca Tarigo, Nicolo Zeno* (1928); *Alvise da Mosto, Antonio da Noli, Lanzerotto Malocello, Leon Pancaldo, Emanuele Pessagno, Antonio Pigafetta, Antoniotto Usodimare, Ugolino Vivaldi* (1929); *Nicoloso da Recco* (1930)		

SPECIFICATION		
Class: Soldati (destroyer) Data 1st Group as completed		
Displacement: 1,715 tons (2,290 tons full load)		
Length: 341ft (103.9m) pp, 350ft (106.7m) oa		
Beam: 33.5ft (10.2m)		
Draught: 11.5ft (3.5m)		
Machinery: 3 boilers, geared turbines, 2 shafts, 50,000shp		
Speed: 39kt		
Range: n/a		
Complement: 219		
Protection: nil		
Armament: Guns: 4 4.7in/119mm (2 × 2), 1 4.7in/15 starshell, 1 37mm/1.45in AA, 8 or 12 20mm/0.8in AA (8/12 × 1). Torpedoes: 6 21in (533mm) torpedo tubes (2 × 3).		
Aircraft: nil		
Ships in Class: 1st Group: *Artigliere, Aviere, Camicia Nera* (1937); *Alpino, Ascari, Bersagliere, Carabiniere, Corazziere, Fuciliere, Geniere, Granatiere, Lanciere* (1938). 2nd Group: *Corsaro, Legionario, Mitragliere, Velite* (1941); *Bombardiere, Squadrista* (1942).		

Minikaze/Kamikaze/Mutsuki

The Mutsuki class destroyers were the first to be armed with the potent 24in (610mm) Long Lance torpedo. (US Navy Historical Branch)

Ordered in 1923, the Mutsuki group of 12 'First Class' destroyers was the culmination of a series of relatively conventional destroyers built in the immediate aftermath of World War I as Japan sought to bring her navy up to front-rank status. Their immediate predecessors were the Minikaze and Kamikaze classes and all were basically very similar, being armed with four 4.7in (119mm) guns and three sets of twin torpedo tubes, although an unusual feature was that the forward set of tubes was mounted in a well deck forward of the bridge, giving these ships a very distinctive profile. The Mutsuki class, however, introduced a major innovation in that the standard 21in (533mm) torpedoes on the earlier classes were replaced by the new 24in (610mm) 'Long Lance' in two triple mountings. These carried a 795lb (360kg) warhead with ranges up to 22,000 yards (20,120m), well over double that of conventional torpedoes. In the early stages of the war, when the Allies were unaware of the potentialities of this weapon, several warships were lost because it was assumed that they were safely beyond the range of torpedo attack. In 1941–2 most of the Mutsuki class were modified to act as fast transports. The light AA armament was progressively increased so that surviving vessels in 1944 carried up to 20 25mm (1in) guns as well as several 13mm (0.5in) machine guns. This entailed the removal of two 4.7in guns and also the minesweeping and minelaying gear. None of the class survived the war, many being lost in the fierce naval campaign fought around the Solomon Islands up to 1943.

Yuzuki, a Mutsuki class destroyer launched in 1927. The bow number indicates 23rd Destroyer Squadron. (Maritime Photo Library)

SPECIFICATION

Class: Minikaze/Kamikaze/Mutsuki (destroyer) Data Mutsuki class
Displacement: 1,313 tons (1,445 tons full load)
Length: 320ft (97.5m) pp, 336ft (102.4m) oa
Beam: 30ft (9.1m)
Draught: 13ft (4m) (mean)
Machinery: Kanpon geared turbines, 2 shafts, 38,500shp
Speed: 37kt
Range:
Complement: 150
Protection: nil
Armament: Guns: 4 4.7in/119mm (4 × 1), 2 .303in (7.7mm) MG. Torpedoes: 6 24in (610mm) torpedo tubes (2 × 3).
Aircraft: nil
Ships in Class: Minikaze class: 13 vessels (1919–22)
Kamikaze class: 9 vessels (1922–5)
Mutsuki class: 12 vessels (1925–7)

Amigiri **was one of the second group of Fubuki class Special Type destroyers.** *(US Navy Historical Branch)*

Limited by the Washington treaty to a navy three-fifths the size of that of America or Britain, Japan sought to ensure that individual vessels were the heaviest armed of their type in order to offset the numerical inferiority. In the case of destroyers, this resulted in the 'Special Type' destroyers ordered in the late 1920s, and eventually 24 were completed between 1928 and 1932. The basic layout of these ships was established by the 10 units of the Fubuki class armed with six 5in (127mm) guns in three twin turrets disposed one forward and two aft. No fewer than nine 24in (610mm) torpedo tubes were carried in three twin mountings, one between the two raked funnels and the other two further aft. On a displacement of 2,000 tons, they were large and heavily armed, and their appearance prompted the construction of the Porter class in the United States and the Tribal class for the Royal Navy.

The 10 vessels of the first group were followed by a second group of Special Type destroyers which differed mainly in that a new DP 4.7in (119mm) twin mounting in which the guns could elevate to 75 degrees was fitted, and an associated HA fire-control system was also installed. This was more than a decade before equivalent equipment became available in British destroyers. A third group of four vessels, known as the Akatsuki class, was completed in 1932 and these had three high-pressure boilers instead of the four standard boilers of the earlier ships, and the bridge was increased in size.

The heavy armament and its associated equipment made the Special Type destroyers rather top heavy and as a result of heavy damage sustained by many vessels during a typhoon in 1935, and the loss of a torpedo boat in a storm the previous year, the whole class was extensively strengthened and modified during the late 1930s. During World War II 21 of the 24 Special Type destroyers built were lost in action (another was lost as a result of a collision in 1934).

The last four Special Type destroyers could be distinguished by a slimmer fore funnel, as shown in this view of the Ikazuchi. *(US Navy Historical Branch)*

SPECIFICATION

Class: Fubuki (Special Type) (destroyer) Data 1st Group as built
Displacement: 2,090 tons (2,430 tons full load)
Length: 367ft (111.9m) pp, 388.5ft (118.4m) oa
Beam: 34ft (10.4m)
Draught: 10.5ft (3.2m)
Machinery: 4 boilers, Kanpon geared turbines, 2 shafts, 50,000shp
Speed: 34kt
Range: 5,000nm (9,260km) at 14kt
Complement: 197 (peacetime)
Protection: nil
Armament: Guns: 6 5in/127mm (3 × 2), 2 0.5in/13mm AA (2 × 1). Torpedoes: 9 24in (610mm) torpedo tubes (3 × 3).
Aircraft: nil
Ships in Class: Fubuki 1st Group: 10 vessels (1927–8)
Fubuki 2nd Group: 10 vessels (1929–31)
Akatsuki class: 4 vessels (1931–2)

Asashio/Kagero/Yugumo

Artist's impression of a Yugumo class destroyer as completed with designed armament of six 5in (127mm) guns.

The Fubuki Special Type destroyers were followed by six ships of the Hatsuharu class which introduced the concept of providing reloads for the torpedo tubes, but these proved to be desperately unstable and the design was extensively modified. The next vessels (Shiratsuyu class) were very similar but were completed with all the necessary modifications incorporated. Experience with these two classes led to the Asashio class of 10 destroyers which formed the basis for much subsequent Japanese destroyer construction. Armed with six 5in (127mm) DP guns in twin turrets they were originally completed with eight 24in (610mm) torpedo tubes in two quadruple mounts, each with a full set of reloads. However, the reload facility was removed, as was X turret, in 1943–4 in order to increase the light AA armament. Despite this, four were lost to air attack while another four were sunk in surface actions, and the remaining pair by submarine attack.

The subsequent Kagero class (18 ships) featured only minor modifications to reduce top weight, although wartime alterations followed the same pattern. They were widely regarded as the most successful Japanese destroyers, although only one survived the war, being ceded to China in 1947. The final embodiment of the Special Type design was the Yugumo class of which 28 were ordered but only 20 were completed, and all were lost during the war. Compared to the Kagero class, the elevation of the main armament was increased, radar was fitted from the outset, and the bridge structure was rationalised.

SPECIFICATION

Class: Asashio/Kagero/Yugumo (destroyer) Data Kagero class as built
Displacement: 2,033 tons (2,500 tons full load)
Length: 364ft (110.9m) pp, 389ft (118.6m) oa
Beam: 35.5ft (10.8m)
Draught: 12.5ft (3.8m) (mean)
Machinery: 3 boilers, Kanpon geared turbines, 2 shafts, 52,000shp
Speed: 35.5kt
Range: n/a
Complement: 240
Protection: nil
Armament: Guns: 6 5in/127mm DP (3 × 2), 4 25mm/1in AA (2 × 2), 2 0.5in/13mm AA. Torpedoes: 8 24in (610mm) torpedo tubes (2 × 4).
Aircraft: nil
Ships in Class: Asashio class: 10 vessels (1936–7)
Kagero class: 18 vessels (1938–40)
Yugumo class: 20 vessels (1941–3)

JAPAN
Akitsuki

An impression of an Akitsuki class air defence destroyer. The Type 98 3.9in (99mm) AA guns were effective to altitudes in excess of 30,000ft (9,150m).

This class of destroyer was optimised for the AA role and represented a complete departure from the Special Type design. Displacing some 2,700 tons, they were the largest Japanese destroyers of the war and were unique in that the boiler uptakes were trunked into a single funnel set well back from the bridge where the exhaust gases would have minimal effect on the fire control systems mounted on the bridge. The main armament comprised eight 3.9in/65cal (99mm) fast-firing AA guns. Although on the light side for surface action, they were highly effective AA weapons, particularly as they were backed up by two separate HA directors. Type 21 and Type 22 radars were fitted, the latter including a prominent 'bedstead' aerial on the foremast. The original light AA armament comprised only four 25mm (1in) guns, but this was increased to around 50 guns by 1944. Only one quadruple 24in (610mm) torpedo mounting was carried, but a reload facility was fitted.

These ships were extremely forward-looking for their time and were comparable in some respects with the British Dido class and American Atlanta class light AA cruiser, although the Japanese destroyers were only half the size. They introduced the concept of the fleet escort whose prime function was to protect major units against air and submarine attack rather than the traditional anti-destroyer role, a concept which was developed by other navies in the post-war period.

Although a substantial building programme was planned, only 16 Akitsuki class were laid down of which 12 were completed, while projected orders for another 23 were cancelled before work commenced. Six were lost in action and the remainder surrendered at the end of the war when most were scrapped.

The destroyer Akitsuki *blows up during the Battle of Cape Engano, 25 October 1944. (US Navy Historical Branch)*

SPECIFICATION

Class: Akitsuki (destroyer) Data *Akitsuki* as completed 1942
Displacement: 2,700 tons (3,470 tons full load)
Length: 413.5ft (126m) pp, 440.5ft (134.3m) oa
Beam: 38ft (11.6m)
Draught: 13.5ft (4.1m) (mean)
Machinery: Kanpon geared turbines, 2 shafts, 52,000shp
Speed: 33kt
Range: n/a
Complement: c. 300
Protection: nil
Armament: Guns: 8 3.9in/99mm AA (4 × 2), 4 25mm/1in AA (2 × 2). Torpedoes: 4 24in (610mm) torpedo tubes (1 × 4). Other: 6 DCT, 72 depth charges.
Aircraft: nil
Ships in Class: *Akitsuki, Terutsuki* (1941); *Hatsutsuki, Niitsuki, Suzutsuki, Wakatsuki* (1942); *Shimotsuki* (1943); *Fuyutsuki, Hanatsuki, Harutsuki, Natsusuki, Yoitsuki* (1944)

SUBMARINES

In World War I Britain had been brought close to defeat by German U-boats, but by 1939 many lessons had been forgotten, although the Royal Navy was confident that it could protect the nation's vital sea lanes. There were two main grounds for such optimism, the first being that Germany's U-boat fleet in 1939 was a mere shadow of its former glory, consisting of just over 50 submarines, and most of these were small coastal boats used mainly for training. The second was the invention of Asdic (later known as sonar when American terminology was introduced), a device for detecting and tracking submerged submarines. It was confidently expected that this would enable British destroyers and escorts to contain the U-boat threat and at least keep losses well within acceptable limits.

Both assumptions were quickly shown to be unsubstantiated. German wartime production of U-boats quickly reached very high levels and the Type VII U-boat, although small by international standards, attained a high degree of operational effectiveness. This was much enhanced when German forces overran France in the summer of 1940 and occupied the Atlan-

tic ports, increasing the U-boat's effective radius of action at a stroke. Organised in wolf packs, the U-boats now fell on the Allied convoys, and tactics of surface attacks at night completely nullified the effectiveness of sonar equipment. It was not until May 1943 that Allied counter-measures eventually got the upper hand, and subsequently the German Navy put considerable effort into improving submarine technology. By 1945 they had several U-boat types powered by Walter closed cycle engines which gave very high underwater speeds; most significantly, they also produced the revolutionary Type XXI which, had it been available a couple of years earlier, could well have altered the outcome of the Battle of the Atlantic.

In view of the importance of the German U-boat campaign in determining the course of the war, several U-boat types are described in the following pages. Of course, the Royal Navy also had a substantial submarine fleet, but with the Axis nations operating on internal lines of communication there was relatively little merchant traffic to attack. Nevertheless, they closely blockaded the coast of Europe and scored some successes against

German warships. In the Mediterranean, British submarines fought a successful campaign against the supply routes to Axis forces in North Africa but suffered many losses in the restricted waters of this area which were not well suited to submarine operations. Following the surrender of Italy in 1943 and the successful invasion of north-west Europe in 1944, British S and T class submarines were deployed to the Indian Ocean for operations against the Japanese. However, despite many individual brave efforts, relatively little was achieved as these boats had not been designed for long-range patrols in tropical waters.

On the other hand, American submarines had always been designed for such operations in the Pacific and were much larger boats with high standards of habitability for the crews. Early in the war production standardised on a single type (Gato class) and consequently they were produced in very large numbers. Although 60 US submarines were lost (not all to enemy action), they eventually succeeded in effectively isolating Japan and sinking virtually their entire merchant fleet. This was a major factor in Japan's defeat, and one made much easier because the Japanese Navy steadfastly refused to organise a convoy system for its merchant ships, deeming such tactics to be entirely defensive in nature and therefore not appropriate to the Japanese martial spirit. US submarines also sank over 200 warships, including a battleship and eight aircraft carriers. One of the latter was the *Shinano*, converted from a Yamato class battleship and at the time the world's largest aircraft carrier.

Although lacking America's industrial capacity, Japan also built a sizeable fleet of submarines, many of which were large and capable of extended ocean patrols. They did achieve some dramatic successes, including the sinking of the carrier USS *Wasp* and the cruiser USS *Indianapolis*, the latter just after she had delivered the first atomic bomb to the B-29 bomber base at Tinian in the Pacific. However, just as the surface navy regarded convoys as unnecessary, the Japanese submarine command tended to concentrate on warships rather than merchant ships or troopships and wasted many opportunities. Japan also built a series of very large submarine cruisers, culminating in the enormous I-400 class described in this section. Many of the earlier classes were modified to carry Kaitens, a form of human suicide torpedo which was produced in large numbers in 1944–5, although their operational results were quite insignificant, especially when compared to the damage wrought by the airborne Kamikazes.

An example of an Allied submarine cruiser, the French *Surcouf*, is contained in this section. Space does not permit the inclusion of descriptions of Italian submarines, although significant numbers were commissioned and many served alongside German U-boats from the French Atlantic ports. Although slightly outside the scope of this book, mention should be made of the Italian human torpedoes (in which the two-man crew conveyed warheads to the target and then escaped – they were not suicide weapons like the Japanese Kaiten). These achieved some remarkable successes, notably the disabling of two British battleships at Alexandria in late 1941. This prompted British development of human torpedoes which were used with some success against axis targets, and these were followed by the X class midget submarines used to attack the *Tirpitz* in 1943.

Note: In this section the two figures quoted for speed refer to maximum surface and submerged speeds respectively.

S class

HMS Safari. *(RN Submarine Museum)*

In the 1930s, as the prospect of a European war began to emerge, consideration was given to producing a smaller submarine for use in continental waters. Many of the previous submarines built since World War I had been large ocean-going types such as the Oberons and the River class fleet submarines, the latter capable of 21 kt on the surface and having a large radius of action although standard displacement was 1,850 tons, as much as a Tribal class destroyer. The first of the new S class was laid down in 1931, and it is a tribute to the basic design that modified versions were still being built in 1945. Indeed, the S class was the largest class of submarines ever built for the Royal Navy, over 60 being completed while a further four were cancelled in 1945.

While there were many variations and modifications within this number, the S class were basically built in three distinct groups. The first four boats were completed as designed with a 3in (76mm) gun on a disappearing mounting housed in an extension forward of the conning tower. In the next eight boats the gun was conventionally carried on a fixed mounting and the conning tower was slightly lower in consequence. The success of this arrangement resulted in the earlier boats being similarly modified. The last of these 12 S class was completed in 1938, and production then ceased in favour of the larger T class. However, after the outbreak of war, production recommenced from 1941 onwards, although for a while they were not given names but pennant numbers with Flag P superior (P211–P229). This practice was unpopular, and from 1943 all were named. The wartime production comprised the third and largest group and most were fitted with a single stern torpedo tube in addition to the bow tubes, and this necessitated the extension of the hull casing right aft. Many of the later boats were armed with a 4in (102mm) gun.

The S boats gave sterling service in north-west Europe and the Mediterranean, but in the closing stages of the war many were deployed to the Indian

HMS Sahib *was originally commissioned as HMS/M P212 but was renamed in 1943. Note the stern torpedo tube.* *(RN Submarine Museum)*

Ocean where their relatively short range and lack of air conditioning made them unsuitable for long patrols. A total of 19 were lost to various causes in the war, including *Sunfish*, which was accidentally sunk by Allied aircraft.

SPECIFICATION

Class: S class (submarine) Data S class, Third Group
Displacement: 715 tons (814 tons full load), 990 tons submerged
Length: 201ft (61.3m) pp, 217ft (66.1m) oa
Beam: 23.5ft (7.2m)
Draught: 13.25ft (4m) full load
Machinery: 2 8-cylinder Admiralty diesels, electric motors, 2 shafts. 1,900bhp/1,300shp
Speed: 14.75kt/9kt
Range: 6,000nm (11,110km) at 10kt (surface)
Complement: 48
Protection: nil
Armament: Guns: 1 3in/76mm AA, 1 20mm/0.8in AA, 3 .303in/7.7mm MG (3 × 1). Torpedoes: 7 21in (533mm) torpedo tubes (6 forward, 1 aft).
Aircraft: nil
Ships in Class: 62 completed in three groups (1931–45)

HMS Torbay *was one of the early T class submarines, distinguished by the undulating casing and the forward-firing torpedo tube abreast the conning tower.* (RN Submarine Museum)

The T class were intended as long-range ocean-going submarines to complement the smaller S class. Their 1,100-ton standard displacement was effectively determined by the London Naval Treaty which fixed the overall submarine tonnage allocated to the Royal Navy. Allowing for boats already in service or under construction, this left 16,500 tons, and with a requirement for 15 submarines the arithmetic was quite simple. Although the T class were smaller than many previous ocean-going submarines, their design was such that their operational effectiveness was at least as good, if not better. A total of 55 were eventually completed with progressive improvements made throughout their production life.

The first group carried a heavy torpedo armament of no fewer than 10 forward-facing 21in (533mm) torpedo tubes of which eight were in the bows and another pair amidships. They could be distinguished by a rather bulbous bow casing and an undulating deck casing. The next seven boats had a stern tube fitted and the midships tubes were moved aft and realigned to fire astern. The bow

shape was refined and the deck casing levelled out. The third and largest group, commissioned from 1942 onwards, added a 20mm (0.8in) AA gun on the after end of the conning tower and also received Type 271 radar. The use of welded construction was gradually extended so that the last production boats were wholly welded. This technique also allowed some of the ballast tanks to be converted as diesel bunkers, considerably extending their range for Far East operations.

Sixteen T class were lost in action, all except three in the Mediterranean, a theatre for which they were not totally suited due to their size, although they scored some outstanding successes.

SPECIFICATION

Class: T class (submarine) Data *Tireless* 1943
Displacement: 1,090 tons (1,320 tons full load), 1,570 tons submerged
Length: 245.5ft (74.8m) pp, 273.5ft (83.4m) oa
Beam: 26.5ft (8.1m)
Draught: 15ft (4.6m) full load
Machinery: 6-cylinder diesels, electric motors, 2 shafts, 2,500bhp/1,450shp
Speed: 15.25kt/9kt
Range: 8,000nm (14,820km) at 10kt (surface)
Complement: 61
Protection: nil
Armament: Guns: 1 4in/102mm, 1 20mm/0.8in AA, 3 .303in (7.7mm) MG (3 × 1). Torpedoes: 11 21in (533mm) torpedo tubes (8 forward, 2 amidships, 1 stern).
Aircraft: nil
Ships in Class: 53 completed in three sub-groups (1937–45)

HMS Taku *at speed.* (RN Submarine Museum)

U/V classes

U class submarine HMS Una. *(RN Submarine Museum)*

These small submarines were originally intended as unarmed training boats but subsequently the design was altered to incorporate six bow torpedo tubes (four internal and two external) and a 12pdr gun. Like the T class, the raised casing to house the external tubes caused problems when running at periscope depth and it was removed; subsequent boats were completed with only the four internal tubes and the bow was then streamlined and lengthened. Although the first boats were only just commissioning as war broke out in 1939, their small size meant that they could be produced relatively quickly when the Royal Navy needed every submarine it could get, and some 37 U class were completed by the end of 1942, while total production was 46. Technically these were split into two groups, the later examples having a modified stern to reduce propeller cavitation. From 1943 onwards production switched to the succeeding V

class which was identical in most respects except that the hull was partly welded and more powerful diesels were fitted. Forty-two were ordered, but 20 of these were cancelled at the end of the war.

The U/V class were used solely in home and Mediterranean waters as their short range made them unsuitable for the Far East. However, they earned an enviable reputation and one, HMS/M *Upholder*, sank many thousands of tons of enemy shipping in the Mediterranean under the command of Lt Cdr Wanklyn, who was awarded the VC for his achievements. The downside was that 21 of the hard-working U class were lost, including no fewer than 14 in the Mediterranean. Only one V class was lost, as the result of an accident in the Firth of Clyde. During the war several U and V class were allocated to Allied navies including those of France, Greece, the Netherlands and Poland.

HMS Ventura *was the first V class boat. After the war she was transferred to the Royal Norwegian Navy. Note the more sharply raked bow compared to the U class. (RN Submarine Museum)*

SPECIFICATION

Class: U/V classes (submarine) Data V class
Displacement: 545 tons (660 tons full load), 740 tons submerged
Length: 172ft (52.4m) pp, 204.5ft (62.3m) oa
Beam: 16ft (4.9m)
Draught: 14.75ft (4.5m) full load
Machinery: 6-cylinder Davey Paxman diesel engines, GE electric motors, 2 shafts, 800bhp/760shp
Speed: 12.75kt/9 kt
Range: 4,700nm (8,700km) at 10kt (surface)
Complement: 37
Protection: nil
Armament: Guns: 1 3in/76mm AA, 3 .303in (7.7mm) MG (3 × 1). Torpedoes: 4 21in (533mm) torpedo tubes.
Aircraft: nil
Ships in Class: 46 U class (1937–43); 22 V class (1942–44)

USS Ronquil *(SS 396), a Balao class submarine. Note the gun aft of the conning tower.* (Author's Collection)

During the inter-war years the US Navy built a number of submarine classes, almost all of which were large by European standards and were designed with Pacific operations in mind. The experience gained with these programmes led to the 1,500-ton Gato class which entered production in late 1940, and ultimately over 200 basically similar boats were completed. The generous hull volume allowed excellent living conditions for the crew, with air conditioning, separate eating and sleeping areas, and well-equipped galleys. These seemingly mundane arrangements (necessarily not available on British submarines due to their smaller size) were vital in maintaining crew health and operational efficiency on the long patrols of which these boats were capable. Not that military characteristics were lacking. The torpedo armament comprised six forward- and four aft-firing torpedo tubes, and a total of 24 torpedoes was carried. Gun armament initially comprised a single 3in (76mm) abaft the conning tower, but this was later moved forward and replaced by a 4in (102mm) or 5in (127mm) gun. 20mm (0.8in) AA guns were also added.

Some 73 Gato class were built, but before the last of these was completed production moved on to the Balao class which were virtually repeats of the Gato class except that a forward-mounted 5in gun was standard and fuel bunkerage was increased from 389 tons to 472 tons with a resulting improvement in range and endurance. No fewer than 122 Balao class were built.

The final version of the basic design was the Tench class, which was ordered in quantity but most were cancelled at the end of the war so that only 33 were actually completed. The most obvious external difference in these boats was the positioning of the 5in gun abaft the conning tower and the light AA armament comprised one 40mm (1.6in) and one 20mm AA. In some boats a second 5in gun was shipped forward.

The US Navy submarine fleet was enormously successful during the war, although not without problems in the opening stages, and sank over four million tons of enemy shipping. Total losses (all classes) numbered 60 boats.

USS Queenfish *(SS 383), Balao class.* (Author's Collection)

SPECIFICATION

Class: Gato/Balao/Tench (submarine) Data Gato class 1941
Displacement: 1,526 tons (surface), 2,424 tons (submerged)
Length: 307ft (93.6m) wl, 311.75ft (95m) oa
Beam: 27.25ft (8.3m)
Draught: 15.25ft (4.6m)
Machinery: 4 10- or 16-cylinder diesel engines, 5,400bhp; Electric motors, 2,740shp, 2 shafts.
Speed: 20.25kt/10kt
Range: 12,000nm (22,220km) at 10kt
Complement: 80–85
Protection: nil
Armament: Guns: 1 3in/76mm AA, 2 0.5in/13mm AA (2 × 1), 2 0.3in (7.6mm) AA (2 × 1). Torpedoes: 10 21in (233mm) torpedo tubes, (6 forward, 4 aft). 24 torpedoes carried.
Aircraft: nil
Ships in Class: Gato class: 73 boats (1941–3); Balao class: 122 boats (1942–5); Tench class: 33 boats (1944–6)

Surcouf

The submarine cruiser Surcouf, *as completed. The twin 8in (203mm) guns are clearly visible and the W/T masts are raised. (RN Submarine Museum)*

The Washington Naval Treaty laid down that submarines could be armed with guns no larger than 8in (203mm) calibre. While there was no tactical reason for so doing, this clause seemed to prompt several navies to think in terms of large submarine cruisers, and, on the Allied side at least, the most successful of these was the unique *Surcouf*. Laid down in 1927, she was eventually completed in 1934. Apart from a conventional torpedo armament of eight 21.7in (550mm) torpedo tubes, there were also four 15.7in (400mm) tubes aft, these smaller weapons intended to finish off stopped or damaged merchant ships. However, the main feature was the two 8in/50cal guns in a twin mounting forward of the conning tower, the after end of which was enlarged to form the hangar for a seaplane. The 8in guns had a range of 30,200 yards (27,615m) and fired a 260lb (118kg) shell. Rate of fire was three rounds per minute and 600 shells were stowed in the magazine. In the cruiser role, the *Surcouf* was intended to operate against enemy trade routes and she carried a launch for boarding parties and had a compartment set aside to accommodate up to 40 prisoners.

With the fall of France in the summer of 1940, *Surcouf* was one of the few French ships to immediately escape to Britain with the intention of continuing operations against Germany. She operated for two years in the Atlantic and the Caribbean, where she was eventually lost in a tragic accident, being rammed by the US merchant ship *Thompson Lykes* in February 1942. It is interesting to note that the US Navy built a small number of 2,700-ton submarines armed with two 6in (152mm) guns, but these were much more conventional in appearance, while the Royal Navy launched the experimental X.1 in 1923 armed with four 5.2in (132mm) guns in two twin turrets, although this vessel was scrapped in 1936.

SPECIFICATION

Class: Surcouf (submarine cruiser) Data as designed
Displacement: 3,304 tons (surface), 4,218 tons (submerged)
Length: 361ft (110m) oa
Beam: 29.5ft (9m)
Draught: 24ft (7.3m)
Machinery: 2 shafts. Sulzer diesel engines, 7,600bhp, electric motors, 3,400shp
Speed: 18kt/10kt
Range: 10,000nm (18,250km) at 10kt
Complement: 118
Protection: nil
Armament: Guns: 2 8in/203mm (1 × 2), 2 37mm/1.45in AA (2 × 1), 4 13.7mm/0.5in AA (2 × 2). Torpedoes: 8 21.7in (550mm) torpedo tubes, 14 torpedoes; 4 15.7in (400mm).
Aircraft: One
Ships in Class: *Surcouf* (1929)

A close-up of the conning tower of U-203, a Type VIIC, leaving Brest in April 1943. She was sunk three weeks later by combined aircraft and destroyer depth-charge attacks. (Author's Collection)

The Type VII was the most prolific of the German U-boats in World War II and the staggering total of 721 were actually built. The origins of this class lay in seagoing submarines built to German designs for Finland and Turkey in the early 1930s, and the original Type VIIA was conceived as the smallest possible boat able to meet operational requirements. At that time Germany had nominally agreed to a submarine tonnage restriction, and consequently by limiting the size of individual submarines, more could be built. The Type VIIA was actually very similar in size to the contemporary British S class. Development of the basic design led to the Type VIIB in which the hull was slightly lengthened to accommodate more powerful diesels, saddle tanks were fitted and bunkerage rose from 67 tons to 108 tons. When war broke out in 1939 a total of 10 Type VIIA were in service while 11 Type VIIB were completed or under construction; the total U-boat fleet numbered just over 50 vessels. However, in these early days Type VII U-boats scored some notable successes, including the sinking of the battleship *Royal Oak* at Scapa Flow and the aircraft carrier *Courageous* in the English Channel.

As a result of war experience, production switched to the Type VIIC which carried additional external torpedo reloads and had provision for a heavier AA armament. This was to be the most prolific version, and a total of 616 were built. Subsequently a number of modifications were made including the addition of armour plating to the conning tower and, from May 1943 onwards, the Dutch-developed schnorkel, which enabled the diesels to run and charge the batteries while the boat was submerged. Other versions produced included the minelaying Type VIID with a 32ft (9.8m) hull insert housing 35 mines. Only six of these were built, although a derivative was the Type VIIF in which the minelaying compartment was adapted to stow 25 torpedoes and bunkerage was increased to 199 tons so that these boats could act as supply ships to other U-boats on patrol. Four were completed.

In the North Atlantic and beyond, the Type VII bore the brunt of the fighting, although considerable fortitude was required of the crews as living conditions on board were almost beyond endurance on long patrols, and were not made easier by the diminishing chances of surviving a patrol in the later stages of the campaign.

A Type VIIC (U-230) running at speed on the surface. (WZ Bilddienst)

SPECIFICATION

Class: Type VII U-boat Data Type VIIC
Displacement: 769 tons (871 tons submerged)
Length: 220.25ft (67.1m)
Beam: 20.25ft (6.2m)
Draught: 16ft (4.9m)
Machinery: Diesel (2,800bhp)/electric (750shp) motors, 2 shafts.
Speed: 17kt/7.5kt
Range: 6,500nm (12,040km) at 12kt
Complement: 44
Protection: nil
Armament: Guns: 1 3.5in/89mm, 1 37mm/1.45in AA, 2 20mm/0.8in AA (2 x 1). Torpedoes: 5 21in (533mm) torpedo tubes (4 forward, 1 aft). 14 torpedoes or mines stowed.
Aircraft: nil
Ships in Class: 721 of all variants completed (1936–44)

GERMANY
Type IX U-boat

U-124, a Type IXB, seen from an escorting warship. (WZ Bilddienst)

The Kriegsmarine's first ocean-going submarines were the two Type IA U-boats laid down in 1935 and based on the E1 design built for Turkey. Further development produced an enlarged design with a standard displacement of just over 1,000 tons in surface trim (roughly equivalent to the British T class) to produce the Type IX. They were used mainly for long-range patrols in the South Atlantic, Indian and Pacific oceans and appeared less often in the North Atlantic where the main convoy battles were being fought.

Although produced in far fewer numbers than the Type VII, there were several versions built. The original Type IXA carried 154 tons of diesel fuel giving it a range of 8,100 nautical miles (15,000km) at 12kt. The Type IXB had slightly increased bunkerage and in many of these versions the 4in (102mm) gun was removed and replaced by two twin 20mm (0.8in) AA. The Type IXC had bunkerage increased to 208 tons, increasing range to 11,000 nautical miles (20,370km), and

two of this class (*U-511* and *U-1224*) were transferred to the Imperial Japanese Navy who renumbered them RO.500 and 501. There was a subvariant known as the Type IXC40 which differed only in items of equipment fitted, but a more extensively modified version was the Type IXD1 in which torpedoes and some battery capacity was removed so that they could act as long-range tankers carrying 252 tons of fuel oil in addition to the standard bunkerage. They were also fitted with low-powered diesels, but the subsequent Type IXD2 had much more powerful diesels and a full torpedo armament so that it could conduct a fighting patrol while still acting as a tanker to other boats. In a striking portent of things to come, one Type IX was experimentally fitted with fixed rocket launchers firing a surface-to-surface missile. Trials were carried out in 1942 in the Baltic, including firings while submerged, but these tests were not followed up and *U-511* returned to normal service.

A Type IXC (U-66) returns from an Atlantic sortie. (WZ Bilddienst)

SPECIFICATION

Class: Type IX U-boat Data Type IXC 1940
Displacement: 1,120 tons (1,232 tons submerged)
Length: 252ft (76.8m) oa
Beam: 22.25ft (6.8m)
Draught: 15.5ft (4.7m)
Machinery: Diesel (4,400bhp)/electric (1,000shp) motors, 2 shafts.
Speed: 18kt/7.25kt
Range: 11,000nm (20,370) at 12kt
Complement: 48
Protection: nil
Armament: Guns: 1 4.1in/104mm, 1 37mm/1.45in AA, 1 20mm/0.8in AA (2 × 1). Torpedoes: 6 21in (533mm) torpedo tubes (4 forward, 2 aft). 22 torpedoes or mines stowed.
Aircraft: nil
Ships in Class: 169 built (1938–42). Also 33 Type IXD long-range tankers.

A close-up of a Type XXI U-boat showing the streamlined conning tower with twin 20mm guns in a faired cupola.
(WZ Bilddienst)

During World War II German engineers produced many technical innovations which were well ahead of Allied developments. In the case of submarines, a lot of work was done with closed-cycle (i.e. non-air breathing) propulsion systems. The Walter turbine, fuelled by hydrogen peroxide (perhydrol), was installed in a number of experimental designs, some of which recorded speeds of well in excess of 20kt underwater. However, none of these was likely to be ready for full-scale service in a short time-scale, and following the major defeats experienced in 1943 attention was turned to improving the performance of conventional submarines.

The resulting Type XXI actually turned out to be a revolutionary step and almost overnight made other submarines obsolete and set the standard for post-war submarine development. Traditionally, the German U-boat had been optimised for surface engagements with a wide deck casing to facilitate handling the several guns fitted, and even the torpedoes were fired using a bridge-mounted sight. In the heyday of the wolf packs (1940–2), night attacks on the surface achieved significant successes. With the U-boat now forced to remain submerged, it was logical to optimise the underwater performance, and this was done by producing a new streamlined, high-volume hull with minimum protuberances (the only guns were 30mm (1.2in) AA in faired cupolas in the conning tower) while battery capacity was more than tripled compared with conventional boats. The result was an underwater speed of 16kt, astonishing for the period, and a schnorkel was fitted so that the Type XXI could proceed at 12kt submerged while charging batteries. Although hardly any longer than a Type VII, the hull had significantly more space so that crew habitability was much improved.

Perhaps the most amazing aspect of the Type XXI was the rate at which it was produced in the closing stages of the war, despite heavy Allied bombing. This was due to the fact that it was assembled from eight prefabricated sections produced at dispersed centres. Over 100 were actually completed but, fortunately for the Allies, very few actually achieved operational status. It is interesting to note that the technology involved in creating the Type XXI was actually pioneered by the Royal Navy with the R class of 1917 which were specifically designed for the anti-submarine role and achieved 15 knots submerged. For some reason the potential demonstrated by these boats was never fully realised and they were scrapped in 1923.

SPECIFICATION

Class: Type XXI U-boat Data as designed
Displacement: 1,621 tons (1,819 tons submerged)
Length: 252ft (76.8m) oa
Beam: 21.75ft (6.6m)
Draught: 20ft (6.1m)
Machinery: Diesel (4,000bhp)/electric (5,000shp) motors, 2 shafts, silent creeping electric motors, 226shp
Speed: 15.5kt/16kt
Range: 11,150nm (20,650km) at 12kt (surface)
Complement: 57
Protection: nil
Armament: Guns: 4 30mm/1.2in AA (2 × 2) as designed. Most were fitted with 20mm/0.8in guns only. Torpedoes: 6 21in (533mm) fixed tubes forward. 24 torpedoes or 12 torpedoes and 12 mines stowed.
Aircraft: nil
Ships in Class: Approximately 125 completed (1944–5).

An I-400 class submarine. The hangar door is at the forward base of the conning tower, and the ramped catapult over the bows is clearly visible. (RN Submarine Museum)

Like the US Navy, the Japanese Fleet tended to concentrate on large submarines with extended cruising ranges for use in the Pacific. Consequently most types displaced 1,500 tons or more, with several in excess of 2,000 tons. Unlike the Americans, they failed to produce a standard type suitable for war production and continued to develop different and unrelated classes. Some of these, such as the streamlined 2,200-ton I-15 class with a range of 16,000 nautical miles (29,630km), were excellent examples of their type, but only 20 were built. The Japanese also tended to fit a heavy surface armament to their submarines and espoused the idea of the submarine cruiser, building a number of types armed with 5.5in (150mm) guns and capable of carrying seaplanes or midget submarines.

The ultimate expression of this trend was the massive I-400 class, of which three were completed by the end of the war. On typical loaded displacement of over 5,000 tons, they were by far the largest submarines ever built until the appearance

of the nuclear-powered boats in the post-war era. A large hangar contained three torpedo bombers which were intended for offensive action, not just for scouting, although the rest of the armament was relatively conventional. The aircraft were launched from a fixed catapult running out over the bows from the hangar. Intended for patrols of up to 90 days, the I-400 had a range of 37,500 nautical miles (69,450km) and was one of the first Japanese submarines to be fitted with a schnorkel device to enable the batteries to be charged while submerged. Only the first two were completed as designed, and the third (I-402) was converted to a submarine supply tanker while building. Two more under construction were never completed, and orders for several more were cancelled.

SPECIFICATION

Class: I-400 (submarine) Data *I-400* as completed
Displacement: 5,220 tons full load (6,560 tons submerged)
Length: 380.5ft (116m) pp, 400ft (121.9m) oa
Beam: 39.5ft (12m)
Draught: 23ft (7m)
Machinery: Diesel (7,700bhp)/electric motors (2,400shp), 2 shafts.
Speed: 18.5kt/6.5kt
Range: 37,500nm (69,450km) at 14kt
Complement: 100
Protection: nil
Armament: Guns: 1 5.5in/140mm, 10 25mm1in AA (3 × 3, 1 × 1). Torpedoes: 8 21in (533mm) bow torpedo tubes.
Aircraft: 3 (stowed in deck hangar)
Ships in Class: 5 laid down 1944, 3 completed

I-402 at Kure in 1945. (RN Submarine Museum)

Index